POSTERS

of

WORLD WAR II

КЛЯНЕМСЯ ЗАЩИЩАТЬ ДО
ПОСЛЕДНЕЙ КАПЛИ КРОВИ
ВЕЛИКИЕ ЗАВОЕВАНИЯ
ОКТЯБРЯ!

POSTERS

of

WORLD WAR II

Peter Darman

Pen & Sword
MILITARY

This edition published in 2011 by
Pen & Sword Military
An imprint of
Pen & Sword Books Ltd
47 Church Street
Barnsley
South Yorkshire
S70 2AS

ISBN: 978-1-84884-433-9

Windmill Books Ltd
First Floor, 9-17 St. Albans Place
London, N1 0NX

Senior Managing Editor: Tim Cooke
Picture Research: Andrew Webb
Designer: Phillip Stonier
Production Director: Alastair Gourlay
Editorial Director: Lindsey Lowe

Printed and bound in China

PICTURE CREDITS
All images from The Robert Hunt Library except the following:
Australian War Memorial Art Images: 21, 32
Library of Congress: 49, 68, 74, 77, 117, 121, 122, 123, 124, 125, 126, 129, 130, 131, 132, 133, 134, 135,
137, 138, 139, 140, 144, 145, 146, 147, 148, 149, 153, 156, 157, 158, 159, 160, 161, 163, 164, 165, 166, 167,
169, 170, 171, 174, 175, 176, 177, 179, 182, 183, 184, 185, 187, 188, 189, 190, 191, 192, 194, 195,
196, 198, 199, 201, 203, 206, 207, 208, 209, 210, 211, 212, 213, 214, 215, 216, 217, 218, 219, 223
McGill University Library: 16, 17, 18, 19, 20, 27, 28, 38, 40, 43, 46
Randall Bytwerk: 3, 61, 62, 63, 64, 65, 66, 70, 71, 73, 78, 79, 80, 81, 82, 83, 84, 85, 91
Topfoto: 52, 53, 55, 56, 57

Page 2: A Soviet wartime poster celebrating the achievements of the Bolshevik Revolution.

Pen & Sword Books Ltd incorporates the Imprints of Pen & Sword Aviation, Pen & Sword Family History, Pen & Sword Maritime,
Pen & Sword Military, Wharncliffe Local History, Pen & Sword Select, Pen & Sword Military Classics,
Leo Cooper, Remember When, Seaforth Publishing and Frontline Publishing

For a complete list of Pen & Sword titles please contact
PEN & SWORD BOOKS LIMITED
47 Church Street, Barnsley, South Yorkshire, S70 2AS, England
E-mail: enquiries@pen-and-sword.co.uk
Website: www.pen-and-sword.co.uk

Contents

During World War II, all the warring nations produced thousands of posters to mobilize their respective populations for the war effort. World War II was a "total war," and thus required the total effort of not only members of the armed forces but also civilians on the home front. The poster was a simple yet powerful psychological aid to mobilizing the nation. Cheap, accessible, and ever-present, the poster was an excellent method of reaching every citizen. Whatever message a poster was conveying—patriotism, the need for greater security, increased production—it was directed at every citizen, in or out of uniform. As a member of the American Office of War Information (OWI) stated during the war: "We want to see posters on fences, on the walls of buildings, on village greens, on boards in front of the City Hall and the Post Office, in hotel lobbies, in the windows of vacant stores—not limited to the present neat conventional frames which make them look like advertising, but shouting at people from unexpected places with all the urgency which this war demands."

Nazi and Soviet propaganda

To be effective a poster needed to carry a simple yet powerful message, one that was easy to understand by everyone. Subtlety and sophistication were the enemies of an effective poster campaign. Adolf Hitler, head of the German Nazi Party and from 1933 leader of Germany, was under no illusion with regard to the intelligence of the masses: "But since propaganda is not and cannot be the necessity in itself, since its function, like the poster, consists in attracting the attention of the crowd, and not in educating those who are already educated or who are striving after education and knowledge, its effect for the most part must be aimed at the emotions and only to a very limited degree at the so-called intellect."

This reasoning was duplicated in another totalitarian regime: the Soviet Union. Posters played a crucial part in the development of the Soviet regime, first by helping the Bolsheviks to win the Civil War, and then helping them to mobilize millions of people to fulfill agricultural and industrial schemes in the 1920s and 1930s. The poster campaigns were relentless and blunt, and in case anyone failed to get the message there was a vast internal security organization—the NKVD (People's Commissariat for Internal Affairs)—

to deter any dissenters or slackers. Those who fell foul of the regime were sent to the Gulag, the vast network of labor camps that existed in the hinterland of the USSR. Once there, inmates carried on working to produce the goods the regime needed.

Once the war broke out in June 1941, the Soviets kept on mass-producing posters, but their message changed. The immediate aim was to defeat the fascist invader, though as German armies crashed into the Soviet Union in the summer of 1941 and neared the gates of Moscow, mobilizing the population to save the state itself became of crucial importance.

In the liberal democracies of Western Europe—Britain, France, and the Low Countries—poster designs were usually more restrained than those of the the totalitarian regimes, and indeed those produced during World War I. There were two reasons for this. First, there was the general postwar disillusionment after 1918, particularly after the exposure of fraudulent atrocity propaganda produced by both sides in the Great War. Thus propaganda was most effective when it was least propagandistic. Second, radio, film, and newspapers combined to reduce the overall importance of the poster. But the poster was still important for conveying simple, powerful messages.

Despite their different political ideologies, the Axis states, the Soviet Union, and the Western Allies all produced posters that had broadly similar themes. First was the appeal to patriotism. If World War II was a "total war," then it was axiomatic that each participant had to convince the mass of its population to be loyal to the state. Patriotism was a prerequisite for the creation of vast conscript armies and mass mobilization of those who weren't in uniform. Group loyalty was particularly important in the Western liberal democracies, as their governments were making wartime demands on the population that would not be tolerated in peacetime.

The fight for freedom

Patriotic posters made use of emotive symbols and emblems, such as the swastika in Nazi Germany and the Stars and Stripes in the United States. Many patriotic posters were merely recruitment aids for the armed forces, with state and party insignia repeated on the uniforms worn by the men and women featured in the posters. U.S. posters often added another dimension to the patriotic theme: freedom. This was a peculiar American trait and was lacking in posters produced by other Allied nations, and obviously did not figure in the posters of the totalitarian powers, where individual freedom was sacrificed for the good of the state. For the United States, which even in the dark days in late 1941 and early 1942 was never going to face the prospect of enemy forces fighting on home soil or its cities being bombed by fleets of enemy aircraft, patriotism alone was not enough to mobilize the masses. Freedom, especially freedom from tyranny, is a sentiment that runs deep in the American soul. The promise of bringing freedom and liberating oppressed people overseas was an ideology that many Americans embraced, and helped to convince the American public that the millions of servicemen being sent to Europe and the Pacific were fighting a worthy cause.

The second theme that war posters addressed was that of security, specifically the security of the state and hence the whole war effort. External enemies were easy to identify—they were the soldiers, tanks, ships, and aircraft of the enemy—but internal enemies were more difficult to spot.

The posters addressing security matters had similar wording and images. The most famous was the theme of "careless talk," the notion that enemy spies were everywhere and that a seemingly innocent conversation could be overheard by them, leading to the deaths of service personnel at the very least. Like patriotic appeals, security posters pointed to the need for national unity, with everyone coming together to beat the unseen foe in their midst. Such a campaign may have been effective, but it must have created a home front with high levels of paranoia.

Production posters

A far more positive, and probably effective, poster campaign was that encouraging greater production. It had to be: World War II was a war in which the fighting "teeth" at the front relied on a steady flow of war materials to keep the tanks, ships, and aircraft operating and fully loaded with armaments. This meant civilian populations had to be mobilized to work in factories to produce armaments and ammunition. And the mobilization had to be on a scale hitherto unseen in history. The posters concerned with war production usually emphasized the close relationship between the worker and the frontline soldier, and the dependence of the latter on the former. In the Soviet Union, where people had little disposable income and even if they did there was nothing in the shops to purchase, the emphasis was on mass production—literally outproducing the German enemy in everything. It was an appeal that worked: in 1942 alone the USSR built 25,000 aircraft and 25,000 tanks.

ABOVE: A photograph that not only shows the use of recruiting posters but also indicates the mood of the American public in the months after Pearl Harbor. The location is a U.S. Marine recruiting office in Boise, Idaho, in January 1942, and a member of the public has attached a sign above the recruiting poster. The original caption to the picture stated: "Perplexed is Sergeant Delbert Myers. He doesn't know who attached the sign to the Marine recruiting poster here. But he's not mad. He'd like to congratulate the guilty party."

A fourth poster theme in the war was that of the international crusade. At first the Axis nations—Germany, Italy, and Japan—seemed to have the advantage. In the first two years of the war this alliance was very successful on the battlefield, both in Europe and Asia. But after 1942, with the German defeat at Stalingrad, the entry of the United States in the war, and the subsequent Japanese defeat at Midway in June 1942, plus Allied victory at El Alamein in North Africa, the Axis alliance did not appear so all-conquering. It was the Grand Alliance, comprising the USSR, Britain, and the United States, which was actually the stronger, and the posters produced stressing the alliance emphasized the point.

The final poster category emphasized fear of the enemy. The most extreme form of this strand was Nazi Germany's anti-Semitism. Close behind anti-Semitism was the Nazi poster campaign against the Slavs of Eastern Europe and the Soviet Union. The Soviet Union was the worst of all places in Nazi eyes, as it was populated by "subhuman" Slavs and was the center of the "Bolshevik-Jewish conspiracy." Ironically, the only other nation to employ an overtly racial theme in its posters was the United States. In posters the Japanese were portrayed as rat-like vermin. Americans were in no mood to show the Japanese any mercy following their treacherous attack on Pearl Harbor in December 1941.

chapter 1

British & Commonwealth Posters

german aggression in the 1930s, specifically the takeover of Austria and Czechoslovakia in 1938–1939, prompted the British Government to establish the Department of Propaganda to the Enemy and Enemy Controlled Territories, later converted into the Department for Enemy Propaganda. The Ministry of Information, which was to coordinate domestic propaganda in Britain during World War II, also appeared in 1939.

Following the outbreak of war in September 1939, the British set up four government propaganda organizations: the Ministry of Information, the Political Warfare Executive, the Political Intelligence Department, and the British Broadcasting Corporation (BBC). Of these, the Ministry of Information had the task of sustaining civilian morale. As such, it was responsible for producing propaganda posters, so-called "weapons on the wall," both for itself and for other branches of the government. As in other combatant nations, British wartime posters were often used as part of a coordinated campaign that also made use of film, radio broadcasts, pamphlets, and articles and advertisements in newspapers and magazines.

British poster artists

The individuals responsible for designing posters came from a wide variety of backgrounds, and included academics, writers, journalists, and lawyers. Their work was placed on street hoardings, inside shops, bars, factories, barracks, and offices. Britain's only official war poster designer was Abram Games, who created more than 100 posters. Among the most famous was the simple yet effective "Dig For Victory," a message so essential for an island nation whose lifeline to the United States was being threatened by German U-boats in the Atlantic. He worked with a small staff in an attic in the War Office. For his efforts in the war he was awarded the Order of the British Empire (OBE) in 1958. Another well-known poster artist was Cyril Kenneth Bird, who worked under the pseudonym Fougasse. During the war he was the art editor at *Punch* magazine. His cartoon-style poster campaign "Careless Talk Costs Lives" was among the most famous of the war, and he undertook a wide range of other wartime work for the government, including books, booklets, pamphlets, press advertisements, and even a film strip.

Involving the nation in the war effort

British wartime posters can be grouped into a number of categories. Interestingly, and unlike in World War I, there were no general recruiting posters (male conscription had been introduced in Britain in April 1939). That said, there were recruiting posters concerned with specialist services and others aimed at women (it was realized from the start of the campaign that the female population was crucial to the war effort).

Due to male conscription, Britain desperately needed people to replace the men in all work areas to ensure that the country kept running, especially when it came to the production of munitions. Other British recruiting campaigns were linked with boosting industrial and agricultural output.

Many posters produced by the British reflected what the authorities believed would happen. For example, the government believed that London would be bombed, even gassed, as soon as the war broke out, and so began an immediate evacuation of women and children to rural areas (it was a false alarm, and so most returned). After the fall of France in June 1940, the threat of German air raids became a reality, and 600,000 children were evacuated from the capital. Indeed, by the end of 1940 only one child in six remained in London, the rest having been evacuated, some for a third or fourth time. In addition, Britain became home to thousands of civilian refugees from Denmark, Norway, the Low Countries, and France, all of whom had to be clothed, housed, and found work.

Conserving food supplies

The reality of war soon hit home when rationing was introduced in January 1940, and posters extolling the virtues of thrift and growing one's own vegetables appeared all over the country. As an island dependent on the sea lanes for the import of food and raw materials, Britain was particularly vulnerable to enemy blockade. The first foods to be rationed, in January 1940, were sugar, butter, and ham. Two months later it was meat, and in July tea, margarine, and cooking fats were added to the list. Parallel to the rationing came a poster campaign and regulations to counter the waste of food. In addition, efforts were made to encourage people to eat balanced diets to reduce the likelihood of contracting diseases stemming from malnutrition.

British propaganda was also directed at involving all of the population in the war effort. The work of the Women's Voluntary Services (WVS), for example, was crucial in the early years of the war, especially during the Blitz when German bombers were attacking many

ABOVE: The destruction of the Spanish town of Guernica by German aircraft during the Spanish Civil War (1936–1939) had demonstrated the power of modern bombers. The government feared that German bombers would drop not only bombs on British cities, but also poison gas. Therefore, gas masks were issued to all citizens following the outbreak of war. This Ministry of Home Security poster urged people to carry their gas masks at all times.

towns and cities. The WVS fed bombed-out families in emergency centers, ran clothing exchanges, information bureaus, and rest centers. They also helped people understand their ration books, cared for returned prisoners of war or foreign refugee children, and served thousands of daytime meals to workers across the country. WVS members also distributed a staggering 1.5 million meat pies each week to British workers.

Air attack featured large in posters during the early part of the war, with people being warned to always carry their gas masks, send their children to the countryside, and the location of the nearest rest center.

Digging for victory

The poster campaign to encourage everyone to "dig for victory" (though in 1940–1941 a more apt phrase would be "dig for survival") undoubtedly worked. With Britain importing only half the food the population required, more rural land was cultivated than before the war. In the cities, parks and other open spaces were given over to growing vegetables, and individual citizens had their own "victory gardens" where small amounts of foodstuffs were cultivated. In the countryside, the ploughing and cultivating was carried out by another group who would be crucial to the war effort: the Women's Land Army (WLA). Members of the WLA, who at first faced hostility from many farmers who believed they could not do farm work, undertook such back-breaking work as clearing ditches, felling trees, and driving horse-drawn ploughs. By the end of 1943, there were 75,000 young women in the WLA.

Mention should also be made of those women who served in the armed forces during the war, in the ranks of the Women's Royal Naval Service, the Auxiliary Territorial Service, and the Women's Auxiliary Air Force. Their contribution released men for other duties. Lastly, attention should be drawn to the efforts of civilian and military nurses, who universally displayed a devotion above and beyond the call of duty.

As in Axis countries, in Britain the authorities waged a campaign against those who might seriously harm the war effort. Chatterbugs, those who spread alarm and despondency, and rumor mongers were targeted especially. Most famously, people were warned that "careless talk costs lives," and therefore were urged not to talk about anything that might compromise military operations and convoy sailings. Ironically, German espionage operations in Britain were a fiasco, but the message given out by security posters was a powerful one and made everyone be on their guard against the "unseen enemy." They were also a powerful way to get the whole population involved in the war effort, by making the individual think that everything he or she might say could have a crucial bearing on the outcome of the conflict.

Raising revenue was also crucial to the maintenance of the British war effort. The posters urging savings and government bonds often featured images of babies, sometimes being menaced by the enemy. This conveyed the message that the war was being fought not only to secure victory in the present, but to lay the foundations for a better future. In the case of Britain this was undoubtedly the case, for in 1941 the government commissioned a report into the ways that the country should be rebuilt after the war. The result was the Beveridge Report of 1942, which recommended that the government should find ways of fighting the five "Giant Evils" of "Want, Disease, Ignorance, Squalor, and Idleness." This led directly to the postwar establishment of the welfare state.

The moral crusade

Unsurprisingly, Adolf Hitler figured in many British posters during the war. Dislike of Hitler and Nazism was the one certain thing that bound the people of Britain together. The view that Britain and the Commonwealth were fighting a moral crusade to rid the world of the evils of Hitlerism was a powerful motivating factor for the British. Winston Churchill summed it up when he said: "We have but one aim and one single, irrevocable purpose. We are resolved to destroy Hitler and every vestige of the Nazi regime."

It was easy for the British to hate Hitler. After all, during the Blitz thousands had been forced to take refuge in uncomfortable garden Anderson shelters, or in Underground stations in London. After a raid survivors would emerge from the shelters to discover if their houses still stood, and if their neighbors, friends, and relatives were still alive. And the raids went on for weeks, sometimes months. In such an atmosphere it was easy to hate the enemy. Even in 1944, German aerial weapons were still being launched against Britain. In June, the first V-1 flying bombs attacked the British Isles. Some 5,800 V-1s were launched against Britain in total, of which 2,420 hit London, killing 9,000 people. A smaller number of the V-2 rocket, 517, landed on London.

When German bombs were raining down on British towns and cities, it was easy to mobilize the moral commitment of the population. Indeed, the fortitude of the people during the Battle of Britain and the Blitz established a theme of British invincibility and resolution for the rest of the war.

The British Empire

When discussing British participation in World War II, mention must also be made of the colonies of the Empire and the nations of the Commonwealth. When war broke out in 1939, the British Empire held sway over a population approaching 500 million people, around a quarter of the world's population, and covered more than 20 percent of the world's total land mass. The countries of Canada, Australia, New Zealand, and South Africa enjoyed "Dominion status," which meant that each had full self-government. And whereas most British colonies were not consulted when Britain declared war on their behalf in September 1939, for the most part each Dominion state individually decided when and how it would enter the war. When war when war broke out in Europe in September 1939, Australia, Canada, and New Zealand immediately sided with the British. On September 1, 1939, the South African prime minister was Barry Herzog, the leader of the anti-British National Party. He wanted to keep South Africa neutral. However, he was deposed by his party on September 4 and replaced by Jan Smuts, who upon becoming prime minister officially declared war on Germany.

The commitment of the British colonies during the war was equally impressive. Some 500,000 Africans, more than 7,000 Caribbean people, and a total of 2.5 million Indians fought for Britain during the war. The British Government recognized the importance of harnessing the manpower of the Empire. In 1944, a government propaganda directive emphasized that "the aim must be to present a picture of the moral and material strength of Britain and the Empire designed to arouse not only admiration and goodwill but also a sense of pride in membership of the Empire."

OPPOSITE PAGE: This Ministry of Information bulletin was the first ever to be issued in Britain during the war. It was issued in Coventry, which was attacked by 500 German bombers on the night of November 14, 1940. They dropped 30,000 incendiaries, 500 tons (508 tonnes) of high explosives, 50 land mines, and 20 oil mines non-stop for 11 hours. The result was 554 dead and 865 injured.

MINISTRY of INFORMATION
BULLETIN

The following information has been prepared at the request of the Government and Local Departments concerned :—

Help your Neighbours with Water.—Will all householders who now have a supply of water please chalk up the words WATER HERE on the door or walls so that neighbours who are less fortunate may be given supplies.

Advice Bureaux.—The Citizens' Advice Bureau is now open as the Rotary Club Room, Liberal Club, Union Street, Coventry, and advice will be given free between the hours of 10.0 a.m. and 4.0 p.m. every day, Sundays included. From Saturday a second bureau will be open during the same hours on week days but not on Sundays at Radford Vicarage, Cheveral Avenue.

These bureaux provide information on all matters arising out of the present emergency.

Fire Equipment.—If any member of the general public sees any fire hose or any other fire equipment not in use, will they please report the matter to the Central Fire Station or the Central Police Station when arrangements will be made to collect it.

Vouchers for Evacuees.—Parents wishing to remain in Coventry, but who have relatives living outside the area, in whose company they can send their children under school age, should enquire at the Education Office, Council House, where travel vouchers can be issued.

Air Raid Casualties.—All air raid damage incidents and particularly public shelters have been thoroughly investigated and there is no ground for believing that large numbers of bodies remain to be recovered. It is pure rumour and to believe it is playing Hitler's game.

To Motorists.—Will motorists please park their cars off the streets wherever possible. Vehicles should not be driven into the centre of the City if it can be avoided, and they must NOT be parked in this area unless urgently required for official duties. Your co-operation in this matter is urgently requested.

Emergency Petrol.—Applicants for emergency petrol obtainable at the Council House, Hay Lane, Coventry, must produce their registration books or insurance certificates, or road fund licences.

This office will be closed on Monday the 25th inst., at 3.0 p.m., and all subsequent applications for emergency petrol by persons employed by firms engaged on work of national importance must be made to the Divisional Petroleum Officer, Birmingham, through their employers.

Tips to Shelter Users.—If you use a shelter, you can help largely in preventing illness within it. Here are some tips :

Help keep the shelter and sanitary accommodation clean.
Provide yourself with warm covering as far as you can.
Do not overcrowd sleeping space.
Gargle daily night and morning.
Bring a handkerchief and always cough or sneeze in it.
Form your own shelter committee to promote the above.

Children are better in the country than in town shelters. Evacuate your children if possible.

Coal.—All Coventry merchants have good supplies of household coal. They will especially give preference to small consumers—two bags per house—before supplying larger households who have stocks.

TRAVEL PERMITS.

Eire.—No person can go to Eire without a permit. No person between the ages of 16 and 60 can receive a permit.

Persons under 16 or over 60 must apply to the travel permit office, 36 Dale Street, Liverpool. No travel vouchers or other assistance can be given.

Discussions with the High Commissioner for Eire are proceeding with a view to Eire accepting women and children but no arrangements have yet been made.

Northern Ireland.—Mothers with children under five years of age are received in Northern Ireland if they can satisfy the Evacuation Officer that they have been able to make their own arrangements for reception in that country. Such mothers can take with them children of school age also.

Application should be made to the Education Officer, Council House.

Scotland.—Arrangements are the same as for England and Wales.

No Typhoid in Coventry.—There is no typhoid in Coventry, and the precautions being undertaken by the Medical Officer of Health are simply to ensure that there shall be no such cases.

Hot Meals.—Hot meals are now available at the Technical College. The main course is priced at 6d., sweets costing 2d. and tea 1d. Further centres will be opened shortly.

Volunteers for Rest Centres.—Those who desire to render full time voluntary assistance at Rest Centres should apply to the W.V.S. Welfare Centre, Gulson Road. Voluntary workers are also needed (preferably with canvassing experience) for the survey of available accommodation. Homeless people should be urged to apply at the Rest Centres for help and advice.

Coventry Education Committee.—The following students will attend at the Technical College as from Monday next, 25th November.

Senior day students, Army trainees, afternoon domestic students, and students of the Junior Technical, Junior Commercial, and Senior and Junior Art Students.

Sites for Temporary Shops.

The Corporation of Coventry offer vacant sites for temporary shops of asbestos and timber framing in Corporation Street (from the Gas Department Showrooms to Fretton Street) and from Mills and Mills premises to the corner of Hill Street, and also on Trinity Street. Dispossessed shopkeepers in all areas, especially those engaged in essential trades, are invited to communicate with the City Treasurer at the Council House, expressing their wishes for or against re-opening by them on the new sites of a shop for a retail trade.

Shopkeepers who would like to re-open on their existing sites in the outlying areas should communicate with the City Engineer and get advice as to the best way of re-opening.

DENNIS MORRIS,
Regional Information Officer.

22nd November, 1940.

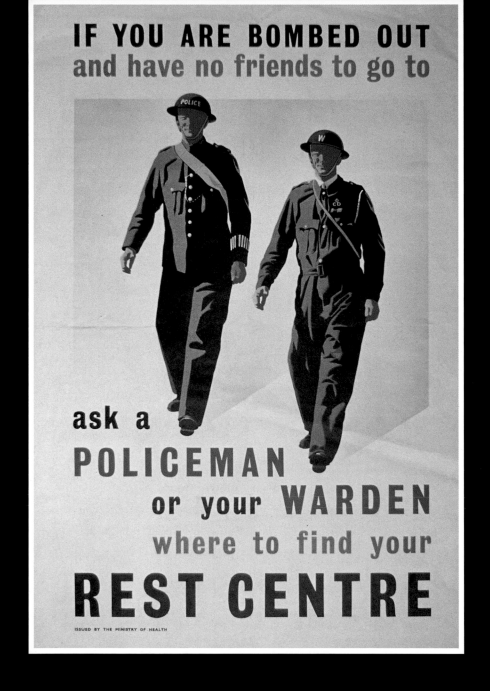

IF YOU ARE BOMBED OUT
and have no friends to go to

ask a
POLICEMAN
or your **WARDEN**
where to find your
REST CENTRE

ISSUED BY THE MINISTRY OF HEALTH

OPPOSITE PAGE: This Ministry of Health poster depicts Adolf Hitler trying to persuade a mother to take her children back to London. The outlines of St. Paul's Cathedral and Big Ben can be seen in the far right distance, together with barrage balloons floating over the city. This poster campaign was not a great success. As soon as war broke out in September 1939, millions of British children were evacuated from ports and cities, designated "Evacuable Areas," to rural locations called "Reception Areas." When the German bombing campaign failed to materialize, most evacuees returned home, only to depart again a year later when the Luftwaffe attacked Britain. Many child evacuees were away from their families for up to five years, and a small minority were

ABOVE: This Ministry of Health poster shows a full-length illustration of a policeman and an Air Raid Precaution (ARP) warden walking together, with the former slightly higher than the latter. Emergency Rest Centers were set up in every town and city that was bombed by the Germans during the Blitz. They were located in churches, church halls, schools, and cinemas. They provided temporary shelter for thousands of people. In Liverpool alone, over 70,000 people were made homeless during the Blitz. Rest centers were usually staffed by members of the Women's Voluntary Service.

BELOW: Air raid protection duties were a vital part of the British war effort in the first three years of the war. In September 1935, British local authorities had been encouraged to implement air raid precautions, and in April 1937 an Air Raid Warden Service was created. The campaign to recruit Air Raid Precaution (ARP) wardens was a great success: there were 1.5 million by September 1939, including women. They were responsible for maintaining the blackout, organizing bomb shelters, and reporting bomb damage. Most had full-time jobs in addition to their ARP duties.

OPPOSITE PAGE: This 1940 recruiting poster makes use of the famous words issued by Winston Churchill in a House of Commons speech made in August 1940, at the height of the Battle of Britain. "The gratitude of every home in our island, in our Empire, and indeed throughout the world except in the abodes of the guilty goes out to the British airmen who, undaunted by odds, unweakened by their constant challenge and mortal danger, are turning the tide of world war by their prowess and their devotion. Never in the field of human conflict was so much owed by so many to so few."

"NEVER WAS SO MUCH
OWED BY SO MANY
TO SO FEW"
THE PRIME MINISTER

MEN of VALOR
They fight for you

"When last seen he was collecting Bren and Tommy Guns and preparing a defensive position which successfully covered the withdrawal from the beach." — Excerpt from citation awarding Victoria Cross to Lt.-Col. Merritt, South Saskatchewan Regt., Dieppe, Aug. 19, 1942

OPPOSITE PAGE: A Canadian recruiting poster that makes the point that Canada and Britain were side-by-side in the struggle against the Axis.

ABOVE: This poster is one of five posters designed by Hubert Rogers for the Canadian Wartime Information Board. It is a recruiting poster that celebrate

BELOW: "Let's Go Canada! Enroll Now". A poster by the artist Henri Eveleigh produced by the Director of Public Information, Ottawa, appealing to French Canadians. The same image was produced with English wording. The appeal to French Canadians largely fell on deaf ears. Nevertheless, the contribution of the country as a whole during World War II was outstanding. More than one million people, out of a population of 11 million, volunteered to serve. French Canadian recruits numbered just over 180,000.

OPPOSITE PAGE: A Canadian recruiting poster that tries to make a connection between Pierre Le Moyne, a French Canadian adventurer and naval hero of the seventeenth century, with the Canadian soldier fighting in World War II. This is a curious poster, for Le Moyne was a French nationalist who fought several successful actions against the British in Canada. The artist who created the poster was Adam Sherif Scott, who was born in Scotland in 1887 and arrived in Montreal, Quebec, in 1912.

PIERRE LE MOYNE, SIEUR D'IBERVILLE · 1661-1706

Né à Montréal. Capitaine de vaisseau, découvreur des bouches du Mississippi, fondateur de la Louisiane, commandant d'escadre. Mort à bord du JUSTE, dans le port de la Havane, il fut inhumé dans la cathédrale de cette ville. Explorateur, intrépide marin et soldat.

AUJOURD'HUI

Peinture par Adam Sherriff Scott, R.C.A., Notes historiques de E.-Z. Massicotte, archiviste et historien.

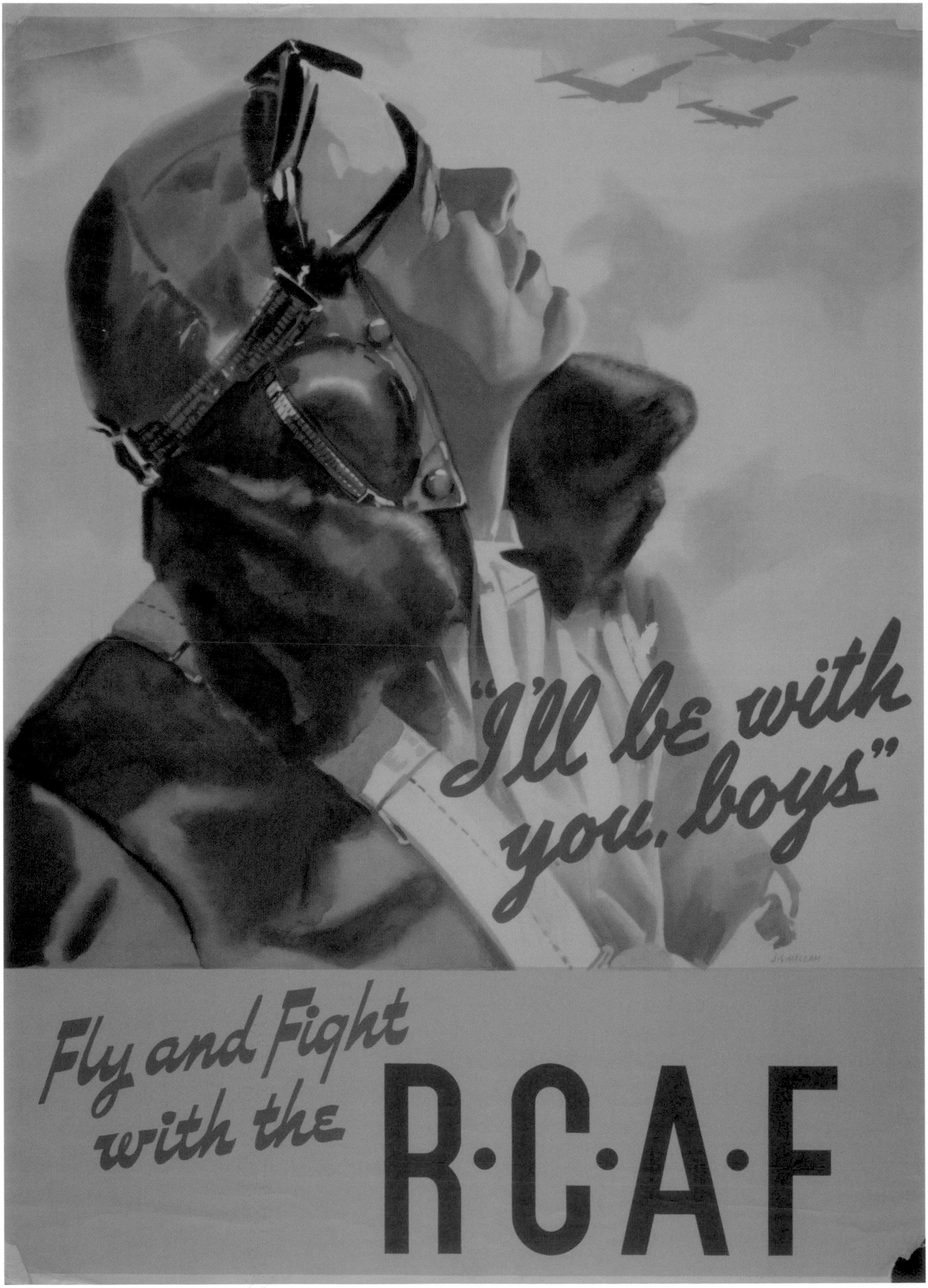
"I'll be with you, boys"
Fly and Fight with the
R·C·A·F

Make dad proud to say . . .
"My boy . . . in the East"

JOIN THE A·I·F

OPPOSITE PAGE: A recruiting poster that was part of a very successful campaign. A the start of World War II, the Royal Canadian Air Force (RCAF) consisted of 4,061 officers and airmen. The wartime total enlistment of the RCAF was nearly 250,000 men and women, of whom 94,000 served overseas. The RCAF also ran the vital British Commonwealth Air Training Plan. By the end of the war more than 8,000 officers, airmen, and airwomen had received decorations from the British and Allied governments, and 17,000 men and women of the Royal Canadian Air Force had been killed in the conflict.

ABOVE: On September 3, 1939, Prime Minister Robert Menzies of Australia announced: "Fellow Australians, it is my melancholy duty to inform you officially, that in consequence of a persistence by Germany in her invasion of Poland, Great Britain has declared war upon her and that as a result, Australia is also at war." During the war nearly one million Australians served in the armed services (navy, army, and air force) or Merchant Marine, otherwise known as the Merchant Navy. This 1943 poster is recruiting for the Australian Imperial Force (AIF), part of the Australian Military Forces (AMF). The AIF was formed in October 1939 as an expeditionary force, and by mid-1940 comprised

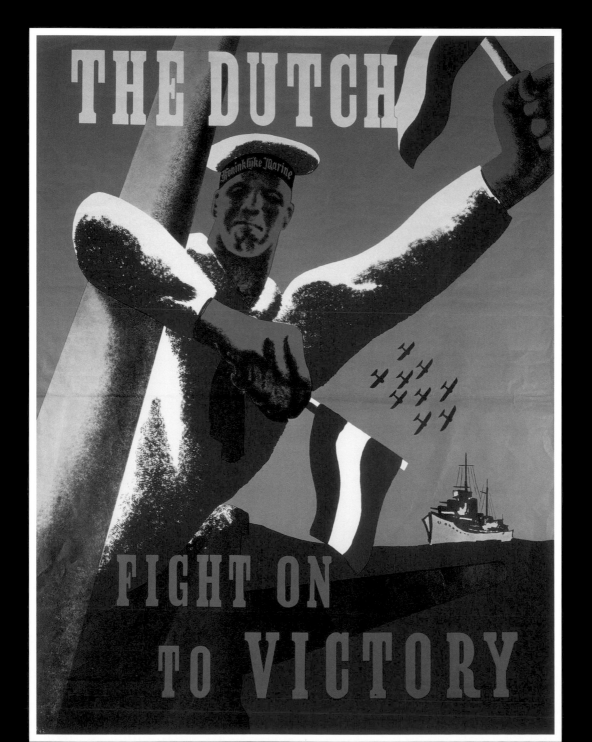

DON'T TAKE THE
SQUANDER BUG
WHEN YOU GO SHOPPING

W.F.P. 301   Issued by the National Savings Committee, London

J. H. & S.   51-3681

DIG FOR VICTORY

Leave rush-hour travel for war workers please

ISSUED BY THE MINISTRY OF WAR TRANSPORT AND
THE MINISTRY OF LABOUR AND NATIONAL SERVICE

OPPOSITE PAGE: The "Dig for Victory" campaign was started in Britain one month after the outbreak of the war. Before the war Britain imported 55 million tons (55.88 million tonnes) of food a year, mainly from the United States and Canada. The government realized that this supply line was very vulnerable to German U-boats, and in any case the merchant ships were also needed to transport troops, weapons, and ammunition across the Atlantic from North America. Therefore the government encouraged everyone to grow their own food. The campaign was a great success. Between 1939 and 1945, imports of food were halved and over 1.4 million people had allotments by 1945.

ABOVE: On September 3, 1939, the government announced that petrol and oil were to be rationed, allowing only 200 miles (320 km) of motoring per month for each motorist. This was to conserve as much oil as possible for the war effort, which was much needed for aircraft and other service vehicles. This restriction resulted in an increased reliability on public transport. However, the buses and trains were already very restricted and undermanned. Posters such as this one therefore asked the general public to consider whether or not they needed to use public transport, and to bear in mind those who might need buses and trains more.

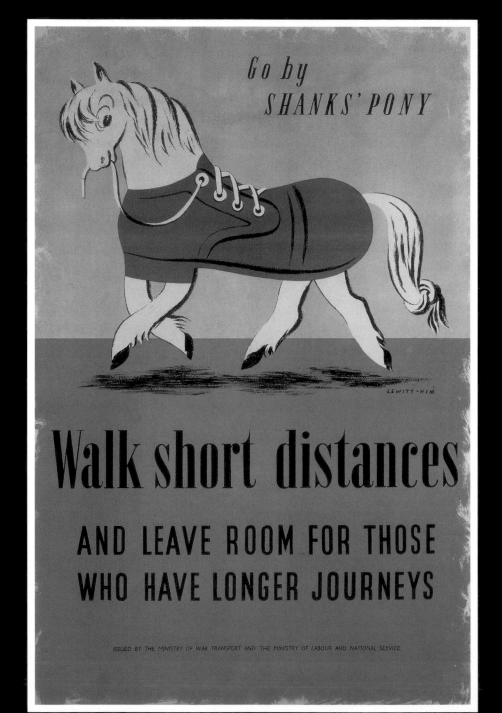

WHATEVER YOUR JOB MAY BE

FIGHT

BIG GUNS OF
THE HOME FRONT

ACTION STATIONS *Everyone*

TREVOR

ISSUED BY THE DIRECTOR OF PUBLIC INFORMATION, UNDER AUTHORITY OF HON. J. T. THORSON, MINISTER OF NATIONAL WAR SERVICES, OTTAWA.   PRINTED IN CANADA 16-4

"We'll have lots to eat this winter, won't we Mother?"

Grow your own
Can your own

OPPOSITE PAGE: This Canadian poster was designed by L.J. Trevor. The war created an unprecedented demand for military as well as civilian goods, as Canada was Britain's principal supplier of war materials until the United States entered the war. To cope with these demands, in April 1940 the Canadian Government created the Department of Munitions and Supply, headed by C.D. Howe. Some 28 Crown corporations were created for the large-scale production of manufactured goods. It was a great success. By 1942, for example, Canada was producing more than 4,000 aircraft a year.

ABOVE: This poster is a variation on the "dig for victory" theme. Under the direction of Lord Woolton, Minister of Food, Britons were encouraged to grow their own vegetables. As this poster illustrates, housewives were advised to make jams, chutneys, and pickles to ens that there were foods in the home through the winter. As well as encouraging individuals to turn private gardens into mini-allotments, the government and local authorities dug up parks, formal public gardens, and various areas of unused land for planting fruit and vegetables. Kensington Gardens in London, for example, dug up its flowers and planted rows of cabbages. The Ministry of Food also printed a monthly *Allotment and Garden Guide* later in the war. It contained handy hints on when and how to plant seeds.

RINGED with MENACE!

BAR THE GATES —
'BEAUFORTS'
So that We may live in Peace

BEAUFORT DIVISION
DEPARTMENT OF
AIRCRAFT PRODUCTION

DON'T HELP THE ENEMY!

CARELESS TALK MAY GIVE AWAY VITAL SECRETS

Opposite page: This 1942 Australian poster was produced by the Bristol Beaufort Division of the Australian Department of Aircraft Production. It reinforces the image of the Japanese as ruthless aggressors, threatening the peace-loving Australians. The answer to the threat is the Bristol Beaufort, a twin-engined torpedo-bomber and reconnaissance aircraft. Some 700 Beauforts of all variants were built in Australia during the war, the first entering service in June 1942. Beauforts were very active in the Pacific, sinking Japanese cruisers, destroyers, and submarines, and bombing inland targets.

Above: When it came to the creation of security posters, designers were faced with a number of difficulties. For one thing, they tended not to use instantly recognizable symbols, unlike patriotic posters. The message that the posters were imparting was also negative, in that they concentrated on the unseen enemy within. This poster is unimaginative in its design and its message is blunt.

BELOW. Another simple poster with a stark message. The "careless talk costs lives" campaign was launched in 1940 and was a great success, the Ministry of Information producing 2.5 million posters that bore the message. As this poster illustrates, the government was particularly worried about merchant convoy security during the war, as the survival of Britain ultimately relied on the supply of food and war materials from Canada and the United States.

OPPOSITE PAGE. During 1940 and 1941, when Britain stood alone in Europe against Nazi Germany, there was a great fear that the Wehrmacht would launch an invasion of the British Isles, either from the sea or dropping paratroopers. As a result, posters such as this one were posted everywhere to enable people to instantly identify enemy soldiers. Some believed that such posters served only to increase the population's paranoia.

'SPOT AT SIGHT' CHART Nº 1
ENEMY UNIFORMS

GERMAN PARACHUTIST

GERMAN SOLDIER

PRINTED FOR H.M. STATIONERY OFFICE BY FOSH & CROSS LTD., LONDON (51/990)

"..... but of course it *mustn't* go *any* further!"

CARELESS TALK COSTS LIVES

BELOW: War bonds are debt securities issued by a government for the purpose of financing military operations in wartime. They are an emotional appeal to patriotic citizens to lend the government their money because the bonds offer a rate of return below the market rate. In this simple poster, the Canadian prime minister, William Lyon Mackenzie King, appeals to the country's workers to buy war bonds.

OPPOSITE PAGE: The British Post Office Savings Bank was established in 1861 for wage earners to save money. The money deposited in the bank, secured by the Treasury, was used by the government to offset against public spending. This was a simple way for the government to borrow money. This poster makes use of familiar images: the British Tommy and behind him the white cliffs of Dover.

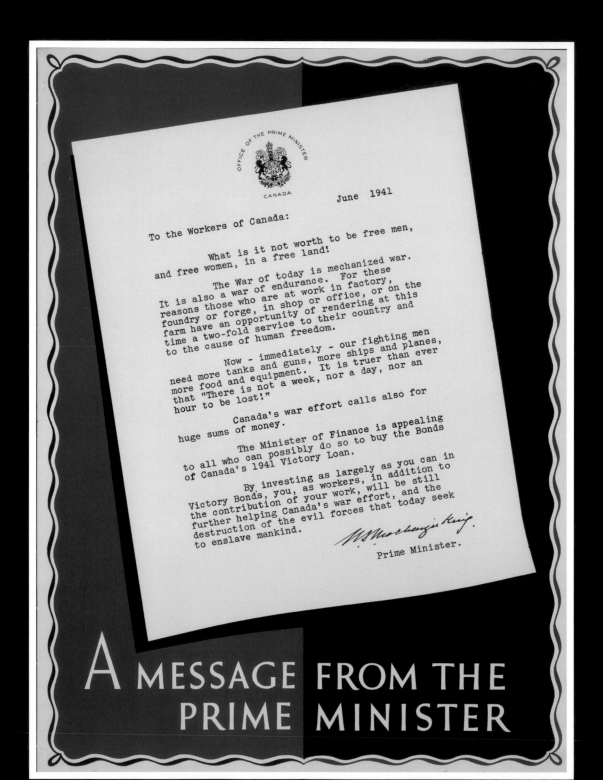

POST OFFICE SAVINGS BANK
FRANK NEWBOULD
SAVE
for DEFENCE
P.B. 30
1394

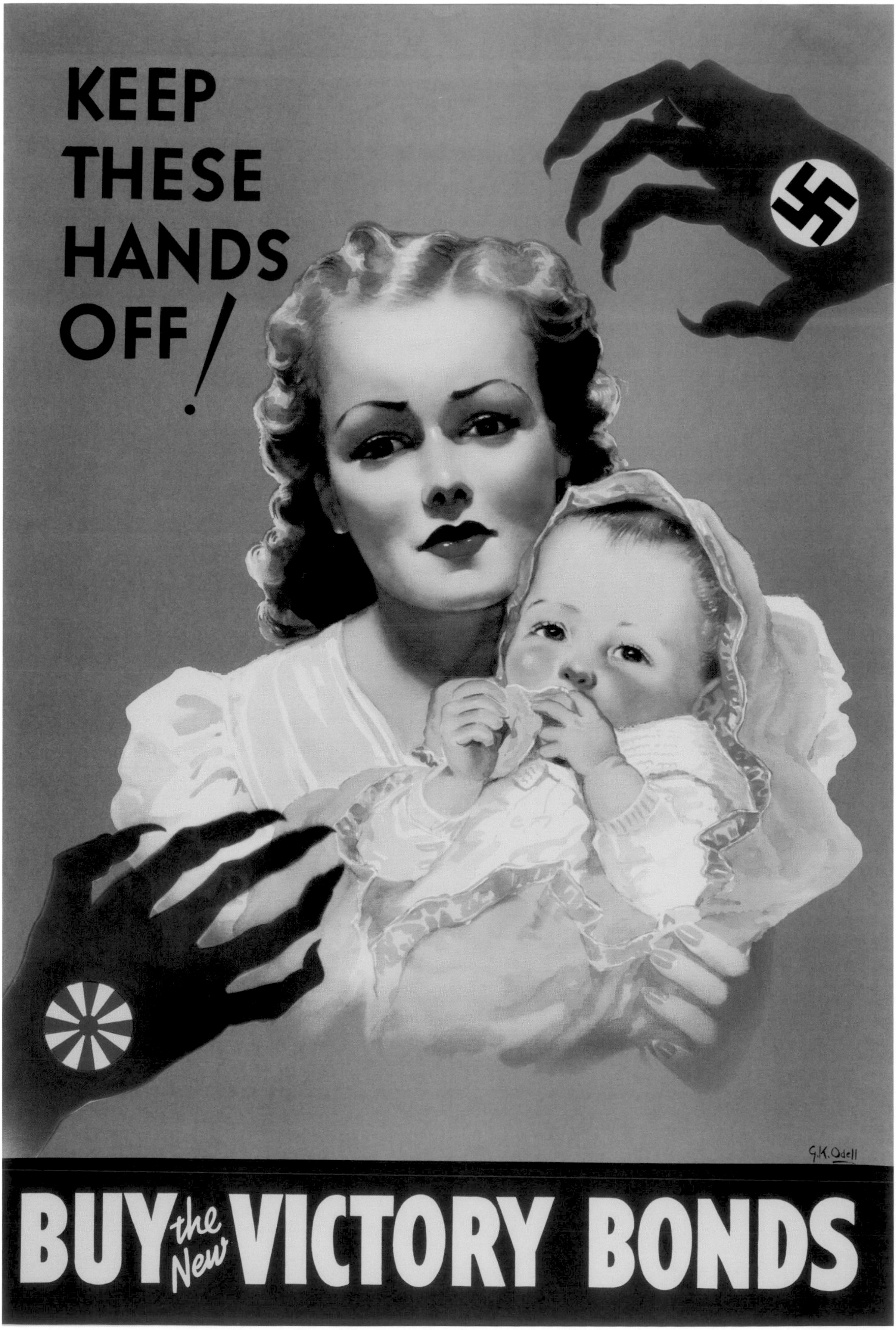
KEEP THESE HANDS OFF!
G.K. Odell
BUY the New VICTORY BONDS

SALUTE THE SOLDIER

BACK THE ATTACK

Victory Loan

massive increase in the number of service personnel after 1939, together with the production of vast quantities of weapons and ammunition, meant that there were millions of people in uniform coming into contact with weapons and explosives. They had to be educated in how weapons and explosives should be handled and stored safely.

A young child is shown against a backdrop of Canada itself. Patriotic appeal is combined with the idea of World War II being a moral crusade to make the world a better place for future generations. The "job" in this instance is to rid the world of fascism, Nazism, and Japanese tyranny and replace it with a new, better world order of prosperity and democracy.

BAD VENTILATION RUINS AMMUNITION

Horse-play WITH WEAPONS

MAY END LIKE THIS···

PRINTED FOR H.M. STATIONERY OFFICE BY WALSALL LITHOGRAPHIC CO. LTD. 51-4950

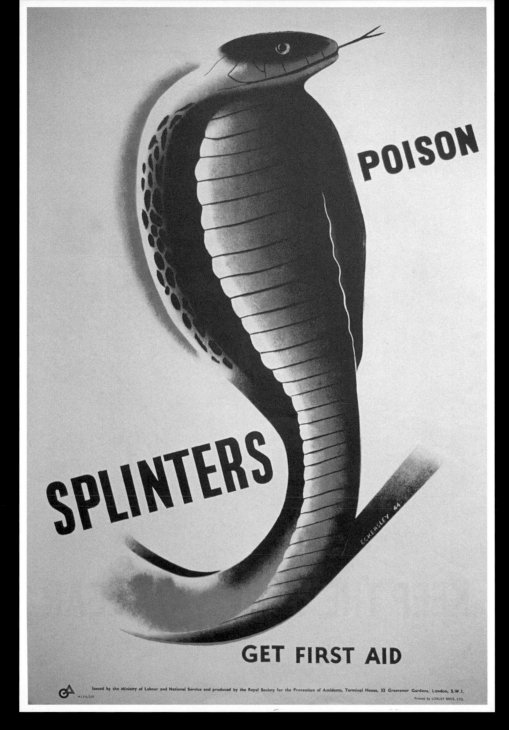

POISON

SPLINTERS

GET FIRST AID

ECKERSLEY 44

Issued by the Ministry of Labour and National Service and produced by the Royal Society for the Prevention of Accidents, Terminal House, 52 Grosvenor Gardens, London, S.W.1.

Printed by LOXLEY BROS. LTD.

Opposite page: Accidental discharges from small arms could result in death or serious injury. The danger was such that the authorities felt compelled to remind service personnel not to fool around with weapons. This poster was created by Abram Games, one of Britain's most important graphic designers. When designing posters, Games stuck to using stark, simple, and thus more effective images. His

Above: One of the health and safety posters produced by the artist Tom Eckersley. During the war he produced propaganda posters for public service agencies including the Ministry of Information, the General Post Office, and the Royal Society for the Prevention of Accidents. His contribution to British poster design was formally recognized in 1948, with the award of an OBE. In 1957 he became

BELOW: This Canadian poster was designed by the artist, author, and architect Harry Mayerovitch. By 1944, Canada had been fighting for five years. The quote by the prime minister reflected the position in the European and Pacific theaters. Italy had been knocked out of the war in mid-1943, but Germany and Japan were still fighting, However, in 1944 both countries would suffer decisive reverses that signaled their ultimate defeat.

OPPOSITE PAGE: A 1944 British poster that shows a Churchill tank, named after Winston Churchill, the British prime minister. In 1944 there were heavy British battlefield casualties following the D-Day landings in France. But the policy of unconditional surrender meant that the country was determined to carry on fighting until the Axis was completely destroyed.

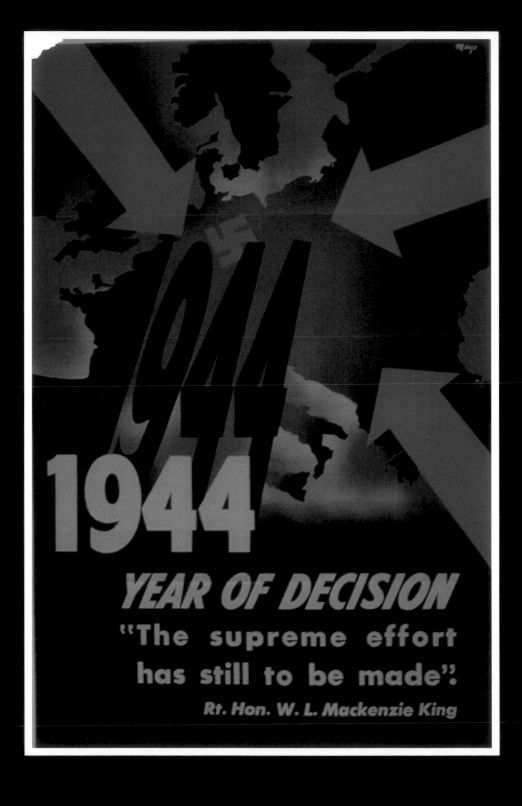

Great Britain will pursue the WAR AGAINST JAPAN to the very end.

WINSTON CHURCHILL

chapter 2

French Posters

france, which bore the chief burden on the Western Front, suffered heavily during World War I (1,357,800 dead, 4,266,000 wounded). It is therefore not surprising that there was little enthusiasm for war among the French in September 1939. Not that the French at this stage were defeatist or pacifist. There was a general consensus after Hitler's takeover of Czechoslovakia in early 1939 that the German leader could not be trusted and that any further Hitlerite demands should be resisted. The patriotic mood was further increased when the Italian dictator, Mussolini, began to make demands for French colonies.

Poor French morale

The swift collapse of Poland had stunned the world, but the British and French in the West were relieved when no German attack was made against them in the fall of 1939. The French under General Maurice Gamelin continued to build up their forces on their border with Germany, bolstered by the vaunted Maginot Line defenses and the troops of their British allies. By May 1940 the Allies on paper were very strong: along its northeastern border the French Army deployed 3,563 tanks out of its total available force of roughly 4,000 vehicles. In addition to this French armor, the British Expeditionary Force (BEF) deployed 196 tanks, the Belgians 60, and the Dutch 40, to produce a grand total of 4,296 Allied armored vehicles in the northeastern theater. Approximately 2.9 million German soldiers faced the three million troops fielded by the Allies.

However, by this time there were severe problems in the French Army. In November 1939, the British General Sir Alan Brooke had watched a parade of French Ninth Army troops. He wrote: "Seldom have I seen anything more slovenly ... men unshaven, horses ungroomed ... complete lack of pride in themselves or their units. What shook me the most, however, was the look in the men's faces, disgruntled and insubordinate looks." Things then proceeded to get worse. The winter of 1939–1940, the so-called Phoney War, was the coldest since 1889, and many units suffered from a lack of socks and blankets. In addition, there was widespread boredom after months of inactivity. All this resulted in a serious drop in morale. This is Jean-Paul Satre's diary entry for February 20, 1940: "The war machine is running in neutral; the enemy is elusive and invisible. Most of the men are fairly receptive to the Hitler propaganda. They're getting bored, morale is sinking." Another recruit, Georges Sadoul, wrote: "End January: militarily speaking we are doing literally nothing. We are so numbed with apathy and cold that many of us do not bother to wash, or to shave."

French propaganda

And what of French propaganda? At the beginning of the war the French had the Propaganda Commissariat, which had been set up by Defence Minister Edouard Daladier in July 1939 and was headed by the writer Jean Giraudoux. The latter had made his reputation in the 1920s producing works that generally denounced militarism and promoted Franco-German reconciliation. Now he had to produce anti-German propaganda. Not surprisingly, the Propaganda Commissariat was a disaster. It was not helped by the government, which offered no guidance as to how it wanted him to present the war to the public.

After the fall of Poland many in France did not know what they were fighting for. The government refused to present the conflict as an antifascist crusade through fear of provoking Mussolini's Italy abroad and conservatives at home—a decision that illustrated the divisions among the French people.

Internal divisions

Like all European countries, France had been hit hard by the Great Depression in 1929. This resulted in political instability (there were six governments between June 1932 and February 1934) and the emergence of right-wing organizations called the "Leagues". In response the communists and socialists signed a unity pact in June 1934 (the communists had been ordered by Soviet leader Stalin not to destabilize France as he wanted an alliance with Western powers to counter the threat of Hitler in Germany). The left-wing alliance in France was called the Popular Front, and once in power after May 1936 France was gripped by mass industrial action. The legacy of the Popular Front was a right-wing hatred of the Communist Party, and the fear that France would become a satellite of the Soviet Union. These divisions did not disappear when war broke out in September 1939.

It is no exaggeration to say that by May 1940 a general sense of defeatism permeated the French armed forces. The situation was not made any better by the dire state of the army's training. For example, it was estimated in 1930 that around 18 percent of riflemen in an average regiment had never fired a rifle and 25 percent had never thrown a grenade. When the German attack came in May 1940, the French were able to offer only token resistance.

ABOVE: Over 9,000 French volunteers served with the left-wing Republican Army in the Spanish Civil War (1936–1939). This poster is soliciting financial aid for Republican survivors of the civil war and their families. Disagreements over support for the Republicans between the communists and socialists and conservatives in France in the 1930s did nothing to improve French national unity.

Surrender in June 1940 saw the establishment of the collaborationist Vichy regime in the southern half of France, but others vowed to continue the struggle to liberate their country from the Nazis under the banner of the Free French.

The surrender document signed at Compiègne preserved a much-reduced but nominally independent France. The Germans occupied the northern half of the country as well as the entire length of its Atlantic coast to the border with Spain, an area amounting to 60 percent of its prewar territory. The Atlantic coast was to be used by U-boats for raids into the Atlantic against Britain's merchant shipping, if London proved unwilling to reach a settlement. The remainder of France was left to the administration of Marshal Henri Philippe Pétain and Pierre Laval, president and prime minister respectively, who established their seat of government at the spa town of Vichy. The French Army was demobilized and disarmed, although an internal security force was permitted. The fate of the French fleet was less clear and would come to trouble Britain's politicians over the following months.

Vichy France

Vichy France's relationship with Nazi Germany remains controversial. Some French politicians held Nazi beliefs, while others simply hoped to preserve France in some semi-independent form. Nevertheless, the Germans acted ruthlessly toward Vichy, which had to pay for the upkeep of the occupation. The country's economic resources were also exploited to the fullest extent, and some 800,000 workers were encouraged or forced to work in Germany industry.

The French population suffered considerably during four years of occupation. Between 1940 and 1944, the Germans took from France an estimated 220 million eggs, 2.8 million tons (2.84 million tonnes) of wheat, 710,000 tons (721,360 tonnes) of potatoes, and 848,000 tons (861,568 tonnes) of meat. In addition, thousands of cattle were also taken to Germany. One result of this constant looting of the country's foodstuffs was the deterioration of the physical health of the French people. In 1942, for example, it was estimated that in Paris alone the average weight loss per person was 14 lb (6.4 kg).

It is also undeniable that the Vichy Government cooperated in, and initiated actions against, the country's Jewish community, and one concentration camp was actually established on French soil. But other French groups actively resisted the regime. When Germany invaded Russia in June 1941, for example, the Communist Party was reinvigorated and communists became a key part of the Resistance. The Communist Party had been weakened by government repression before the war and had lost thousands of members as a result of the German-Soviet Non-Aggression Pact of 1939. After June 1941 the Soviet Union was no longer an ally of Germany, and so the communists could abandon their view that the war was an imperialistic conflict that was against the interests of French workers.

Collaboration

The German invasion of Russia also caused great excitement among collaborationist political parties and paramilitary formations. In response, the first recruiting center was opened at 12 rue Auber, Paris, while additional recruiting centers were placed all over France. On July 7, all the leaders of these parties met at the Hotel Majestic in Paris to create an anti-Bolshevik legion, and on July 18, 1941, the *Legion des Voluntaires Francais contre le Bolshevisme* (LVF) was established.

Initially the Vichy Government had enacted a law that forbade Frenchmen from enlisting into "foreign armies" to prevent them from joining the Free French forces of the exiled General Charles de Gaulle. Since the LVF was a private affair, Marshal Pétain amended the law so there would be no barrier to Frenchmen enlisting into it. Hitler approved, but stated that membership be limited to no more than 15,000. However, the LVF received a total of only 13,400 applications to join, and of these 4,600 had to be refused on medical grounds and a further 3,000 on "moral" grounds. Many came from the militias of the collaborating political parties. Prominent among these were the men from Jacques Doriot's French Popular Party (PPF), including Doriot himself. Eventually, 5,800 Frenchmen were accepted into the LVF.

In February 1944 the German Navy began to appeal for French volunteers, the main recruiting office being at Caen in Normandy. But, as with other branches of the German armed forces, individual enlistment had taken place before that late date, especially in the traditional coastal regions of Brittany and Normandy. Between 1,000–2,000 Frenchmen served in the German Kriegsmarine in World War II. In France, the German Navy also raised an indigenous naval police known as the *Kriegsmarine Wehrmänner*.

Another separate German naval police unit of French volunteers was the *Kriegswerftpolizei*. This unit consisted of some 259–300 Frenchmen, who assisted in guarding the important U-Boat base at La Pallice near La Rochelle, in the Bay of Biscay. The Allied invasion of France in June 1944 does not appear to have deterred the German Navy from continuing its attempts to recruit Frenchmen. For example, the *Journal de Rouen* dated June 29, 1944, three weeks after the Allied landings, carried an advertisement urging young Frenchmen to join the Kriegsmarine. It stated: "To be a sailor is to have a trade, enlist today in the German Navy."

The Free French

Opposition to Vichy France and the Nazis ultimately centered on the exiled Free French under Charles de Gaulle in Britain, although many ordinary French people initially took little heed of his calls to fight the Nazis and reject the Vichy regime. Resistance grew as de Gaulle's authority and Vichy France's subservience to the Nazis became more clear, combined with the hardships that followed the looting of French food-stuffs by the Germans. The process intensified in November 1942, when German troops swept into Vichy France to prevent a possible Allied invasion from North Africa. Supported by Allied supply drops, French Resistance groups in France grew slowly and undertook a key role in aiding the freeing of the country, though after the Allies had landed in France in June 1944, not before. Regular Free French units also served with the Allied armies and played a part in the liberation of Paris itself.

OPPOSITE PAGE: "One war for one Homeland." A Free French poster emphasizing that the war against Nazi Germany goes on despite the German occupation of France. The Free French Forces (*Forces Françaises Libres*, FFL), under the leadership of Charles de Gaulle, was initially a fringe movement (de Gaulle was indicted as a traitor by a Vichy court for ignoring Pétain's armistice order). However, by 1944 there were 100,000 Free French soldiers in the Allied armies.

LIBERTÉ
ÉGALITÉ
FRATERNITÉ

UN SEUL COMBAT
POUR UNE SEULE PATRIE

N'oubliez pas Oran!

FRANÇAIS

DE 20 A 40 ANS

FAITES VOTRE DEVOIR !

Entrez dans les rangs de la

LÉGION

DES VOLONTAIRES FRANÇAIS

CONTRE LE BOLCHEVISME

POUR TOUS RENSEIGNEMENTS :

Conditions Matérielles, Maisons du Légionnaire, Colonies de Vacances, Service Social des Familles, Bureaux de Placement, etc...

ADRESSEZ-VOUS :

OPPOSITE PAGE: "Never forget Oran!" A Vichy poster. In July 1940, Britain, fearing that France's navy would be seized by Germany, sent two battleships, a battlecruiser, and a carrier (Force H) to capture French vessels at Oran and Mers-el-Kebir, Algeria. After negotiations failed, the British opened fire and sank one battleship and damaged two more. Some 1,300 French sailors were killed in the attacks, and relations between France and Britain sank to a new low.

ABOVE: A recruiting poster for the Vichy *Legion des Voluntaires Francais contre le Bolshevisme* (LVF). The recruits wore standard German Army uniforms and had the French national arm shield inscribed "FRANCE" placed on their right sleeve (the Germans made it clear that unless France actually declared war on the Soviet Union, there could be no question of sending combatants to the front in French uniform). By October 1941 the LVF comprised two battalions: 181 officers and 2,271 other ranks, with a liaison staff of 35 Germans. The LVF was registered as the 638th Infantry Regiment of the German Army. In February 1942, the LVF was caught up in the Soviet winter counteroffensive. It subsequently lost half of its strength due either to enemy action or frostbite.

BELOW: A Free French poster designed for an English audience. In reality, the Free French didn't "throttle the Boche," at least not until after June 1944. Until the D-Day landings France was a relatively quiet backwater, where German divisions mauled on the Eastern Front were sent to rest and rebuild themselves.

OPPOSITE PAGE: "France, beware of the ghosts." A poster by the French League of Purge, led by Pierre Constantini, warning against the spectres of the English, Freemasons, leftists, and Jews. The Nazi influence on this right-wing Vichy poster is apparent—the blonde-haired French girl and the shifty, big-nosed Jew.

FRENCH RESISTANCE
HELPS THROTTLE THE BOCHE

Vient de paraître

Qui est PIERRE LAVAL?

FLAMMARION

2 F.-

PHOTO L.SILVESTRE

AUX COTÉS DU MARÉCHAL
LA DERNIÈRE CHANCE DE
LA FRANCE

V
II — 226
ORAFF
138, Avenue des
Champs-Élysées

AFFICHE D'INTÉRIEUR

Opposite page: "Against communism." A recruiting poster for the Vichy regime's *Milice* (secret police). Formed in January 1943, it was made up of antiGaullists and anticommunists. Numbering 35,000 at its height, the *Milice* specifically excluded Jews from its ranks. It was created to fight members of the French Resistance, who by 1943 were beginning to increase their activities of sabotage and assassination. The *Milice* also took an active part in rounding up French Jews for deportation to the concentration camps. The inverted white ribbon was the logo of

Above: An advert for a booklet about Pierre Laval. It states: "Just out—*Who is Pierre Laval?*—At the side of the marshal [Pétain]. The last hope for France." Laval was a French politician who headed the Vichy Government from 1942. He collaborated with the Germans in an effort to get the best deal for France. In a 1942 radio broadcast he declared his hope for a German victory, "because without it tomorrow Bolshevism will be everywhere." After the war he was found guilty of treason and shot in October 1945.

German Posters

chapter 3

according to one of the myths perpetuated by the Nazis, Allied propaganda in World War I had made a significant contribution toward the German defeat in that war. At the front the army remained undefeated (which was a lie), but at home the civilian masses, influenced by Allied propaganda, became revolutionized and incapable of supporting the army. The manufacturers of Allied propaganda would have been flattered by this eulogy, but aside from it being totally false, it does illustrate a major tenet of Nazi propaganda theory: it did not have to bear any resemblance to the truth. Indeed, lies were a useful asset, and the bigger the lie the better, because the masses could understand and digest it more easily. As Hitler himself had written: "In the big lie there is always a certain force of credibility; because the broad masses of a nation are always more easily corrupted in the deeper strata of their emotional nature than consciously or voluntarily; and thus in the primitive simplicity of their minds they more readily fall victims to the big lie than the small lie, since they themselves often tell small lies in little matters but would be ashamed to resort to large-scale falsehoods. It would never come into their heads to fabricate colossal untruths, and they would not believe that others could have the impudence to distort the truth so infamously."

Hitler on propaganda

Concerning propaganda, Hitler had written in *Mein Kampf*: "The art of propaganda lies in understanding the emotional ideas of the great masses and finding, through a psychologically correct form, the way to the attention and thence to the heart of the broad masses.

The fact that our bright boys do not understand this merely shows how mentally lazy and conceited they are. Once understood how necessary it is for propaganda to be adjusted to the broad mass, the following rule results: It is a mistake to make propaganda many-sided, like scientific instruction, for instance. The receptivity of the great masses is very limited, their intelligence is small, but their power of forgetting is enormous. In consequence of these facts, all effective propaganda must be limited to a very few points and must harp on these in slogans until the last member of the public understands what you want him to understand by your slogan. As soon as you sacrifice this slogan and try to be many-sided, the effect will piddle away, for the crowd can neither digest nor retain the material offered. In this way the result is weakened and in the end entirely cancelled out."

Joseph Goebbels

Hitler and the Nazis made great use of propaganda, especially posters, in the interwar years. The symbols of the party—the swastika, the eagle (supposedly selected by Hitler because he had seen it described in an anti-Semitic encyclopedia as the "Aryan in the world of animals"), and a wreath of laurel leaves—were seen on posters, along with strong colors, usually red, black, and white. The Nazis turned propaganda into a religion, and like all religions it needed a high priest. In 1926 they found one, when Dr. Joseph Goebbels was appointed *Gauleiter* (governor) of Berlin. The posters produced under the direction of Goebbels before the Nazis came to power in 1933 presented Adolf Hitler as the ex-serviceman in civilian clothes who was carrying on the fight as the representative of a nation that had lost a just war. After 1933, Goebbels was appointed propaganda minister and developed the image of Hitler further. Now the Führer was carrying on the work of Bismarck (who had unified Germany in the late nineteenth century) and was about to complete it. One of the most significant posters of the period immediately before the outbreak of war was a half-length picture of Hitler with the accompanying caption: "One People, One Empire, One Leader." Indeed, so powerful was this image that throughout Germany it replaced religious pictures and crucifixes on the walls of offices and classrooms.

The Ministry of Propaganda

Goebbels' Ministry of Propaganda trumpeted two of the central planks of Nazi ideology: space and race. Germany needed *Lebensraum*, "living space," to ensure her survival as a great nation, and a strong Germany also had to be free of "contamination" with inferior races, specifically the Jews (and later the Slavs). The Jews in particular were singled out to take the blame for all of Germany's ills: not only were Jews who lived in Germany enemies of the state, but foreign nations hostile to Germany were portrayed as being manipulated by Jews. Nazi anti-Semitic posters portrayed Jews in the worst possible light: they were shifty, untrustworthy, had animal-like features (thus were less than human), and were parasites. In contrast, Germans were painted as blonde, blue-eyed Aryans who were handsome and physically fit. They were part of a new Germany, one that was establishing a New Order in Europe.

The string of German victories in the first two years of the war, when the Wehrmacht conquered Poland,

Ein Volk, ein Reich, ein Führer!

ABOVE: "One People, One Empire, One Leader." This poster, produced in early 1939 under the direction of Propaganda Minister Joseph Goebbels, was one of the most popular produced in the Third Reich both before and during the war. The half-length portrait of Hitler replaced religious paintings in homes, offices, and classrooms throughout Germany.

Norway, France, the Low Countries, and the Balkans, seemed to confirm the triumph of the New Order. German posters between 1939 and 1941, therefore, reflected these military triumphs. Posters portrayed Germany literally smashing her enemies to pieces, an apt analogy in 1939 and 1940. Likewise, the German attack on the Soviet Union in June 1941 also produced a crop of spectacular victories. German armies surrounded and destroyed Red Army formations as they drove deeper and deeper into the USSR. By December 1941 the Wehrmacht had almost captured Moscow. Almost. However, that month the Soviets launched a massive counterattack all along the line which nearly broke the German Army on the Eastern Front. The Germans now faced at least another campaigning season in Russia, against an enemy that had exceeded all expectations.

War of annihilation

The Nazis reserved a special loathing for the Soviet Union, tinged with fear. According to Nazism, the USSR was the center of the Jewish-Bolshevik conspiracy, and it was loathed because it was populated by those racial groups the Nazis despised: Slavs and Jews. These groups were fit only for two things: to act as slaves to serve a German master race who ruled a Thousand Year Year; either that or be exterminated. However, the Soviet Union also aroused fear, for east of the River Oder resided tens of millions of Slavs who posed a very real threat to the Third Reich. This meant that the war on the Eastern Front was fought with an intensity not seen elsewhere on the European continent. The result was extermination on a vast scale, against Jews, communists, and Red Army prisoners of war. In those areas under German rule, anti-partisan sweeps resulted in thousands of civilians being shot under the vague accusation that they were "bandits." Thus the war on the Eastern Front became one of annihilation between two ideologically opposed totalitarian regimes.

After January 1943, the nature of German propaganda changed. The surrender of what was left of the German Sixth Army at Stalingrad was a catastrophe for the Third Reich. The supposedly "inferior" Slavs had annihilated an army of 300,000 Germans. Suddenly, the Nazis could not say that they were the *Herrenvolk* (master race). They had been both defeated and humiliated. Thus German propaganda shouted a new message after Stalingrad: Nazi Germany was the defender of Europe's ancient civilization against the barbarian hordes of the East. As Hitler declared after the fall of Stalingrad: "Either Germany, the German

armed forces, and along with us our allies in Europe will win, or the Central Asiatic Bolshevik tide will break in from the East over the oldest civilized continent, just as destructively and annihilatingly as it did in Russia itself. Man's efforts, stretching back over several thousand years, to create a civilization would then have been in vain." This remained one of the dominant themes of Nazi propaganda to the end of the war. After Stalingrad Goebbels proclaimed a total war. In a fiery speech made to a specially selected audience in Berlin on February 18, 1943, he railed: "Now, people rise up and let the storm break loose!" As a result of the crisis German women, who until then had not been subject to compulsory work in factories or offices, were conscripted. In German-occupied Europe, further levies of forced labor were raised, and in Germany rations were further reduced.

Most propaganda was fixed on the Eastern Front, which the Nazis correctly perceived as being the theater where the war would be won or lost. Posters hammered home the threat of the "red menace," the "Bolshevik horde," and the "danger from the steppes." Whereas the posters in the early war years had featured determined Aryans, those in 1943 and 1944 portrayed grim-faced soldiers and *Volkssturm* (aged home defense recruits) clutching weapons to face the Red Army. The result of this new propaganda campaign was seemingly successful, in that Germans did resist the Soviet Union fiercely until their defeat in 1945. However, they did so because they did not want to live under Russian rule, and they also did not want to face the wrath of a Red Army bent on exacting revenge for German atrocities committed on Russian soil.

The Hitler Youth

Two other strands of German propaganda should also be mentioned. First, the Nazi obsession with the militarization of German youth. The Hitler Youth organization had one aim only: to produce a generation of German youth that was physically fit, militarily trained, and thoroughly indoctrinated in National Socialist ideology. It succeeded in all three. By 1945 millions of young Germans, both male and female, had served in the armed forces or, if they were too young, on the home front. For those fanatical Nazi youths, there was service with the 12th SS *Hitlerjugend* Division, an élite Waffen-SS panzer division.

Another major strand of Nazi propaganda was concerned with the Waffen-SS. The *Schutze Staffel* (SS) —Protection Squad—was originally formed as a bodyguard for Adolf Hitler. However, by the end of World War II the SS had become a state within a state and its

armed wing, the Waffen-SS (Armed SS), numbered one million troops. The Waffen-SS had its own distinctive creed. This was written down in its training manual: "Obedience must be unconditional. It corresponds to the conviction that National Socialist ideology must reign supreme ... every SS man, therefore, is prepared to carry out unhesitatingly any order issued by the Führer or a superior, regardless of the sacrifice involved." Heinrich Himmler, head of the SS organization, considered that his SS men were unstoppable. He told them, "I must repeat—the word 'impossible' must never be heard in the SS. It is unthinkable, gentlemen, that anyone should report to his superior, 'I can not arrange this or that' or 'I can not do it with so few people' or 'my battalion is not trained' or 'I feel myself incapable.' Gentleman, that kind of reaction is simply not permitted."

Foreign recruits

Although the Waffen-SS was primarily an armed force at Hitler's disposal for the maintenance of order inside Germany, the Führer also decreed that in time of war it was to serve at the front under army command. He believed that frontline experience for the Waffen-SS was essential if such a force was to command the respect of the German people. He also insisted that its human material was to be of the highest caliber.

From June 1941, the Waffen-SS's recruiters were keen to enlist Aryans from outside Germany. The recruitment campaign emphasized the common bonds of the Nordic race, and the threat Bolshevism posed to all the Nordic countries (at first Himmler was interested only in raising legions of Danes, Norwegians, Dutchmen, and Flemings on racial grounds). It was a message that appealed to thousands of Western European males. As the war progressed the Waffen-SS created more foreign units. One, the *Wiking* Division, made up of West Europeans, became an élite unit.

OPPOSITE PAGE: The Central Propaganda Office (*Reichspropagandaleitung*) of the Nazi Party produced weekly quotation posters that were to be displayed in party offices, military barracks, and public buildings. This one states: "National Socialism is the guarantee of victory." It was issued in the fall of 1939, just after the German invasion of Poland. The campaign lasted three weeks and was a stunning success for the Wehrmacht. The quotation posters usually carried the words of senior Nazis or popular slogans, such as "The Führer is always right."

DER
NATIONAL
SOZIALISMUS
IST DER
GARANT
DES
SIEGES

IN DEN
STAUB
MIT ALLEN
FEINDEN

GROSS-
DEUTSCHLANDS!

Mit unfern Fahnen ift der Sieg!

V/18

OPPOSITE PAGE: A very successful poster that was released in the summer of 1940. It literally translates as: "Into the Dust with All Enemies of Greater Germany." In May and June 1940 the German Army had done just that, conquering the Low Countries and France and forcing the evacuation of the British Expeditionary Force from Dunkirk. The German public had rightly been worried concerning war with Britain and France, whose combined might was greater than the Wehrmacht. But the Blitzkrieg campaign of 1940 had been a stunning success and had knocked France out of the war.

ABOVE: "Victory is with our Flags!" This 1940 poster was very popular, and some 650,000 copies were distributed. In Germany the war against Britain and France was packaged to the public as a revival of the 1914 conflict against Germany's "encirclement" by other European powers. The victory over both nations in 1940 was trumpeted as an end to the despised Treaty of Versailles, and revenge for the humiliation of 1918. As such, it gave a morale boost to the German people.

Goebbels addressed the German people: "The homeland and the front form a big family as we bid farewell to a year that was full of challenges, but also of big historical victories.The German people bows in praise before the Almighty, who has so clearly blessed us in the past year by standing by us in battle and crowning our weapons with victory. He knows that we are waging this war for a better peace, that we are fighting for the happiness of people who have so often been oppressed." This poster from the same period proclaims: "*You* are the front!"

OPPOSITE PAGE: A weekly quotation poster dated May 14, 1941, which uses Hitler's words. "No one can get past the German soldier." Though the poster might seem trite, in the spring of 1941 such words were no idle boast. The German Army had conquered Western Europe, Poland, and the Balkans, and in April had again ejected the British Army from the continent, this time from Greece. It did indeed appear that nothing could stop the German soldier.

WO DER DEUTSCHE SOLDAT STEHT/ KOMMT KEIN ANDERER HIN

ADOLF HITLER

HOYER

WOCHENSPRUCH DER NSDAP. / HERAUSGEBER REICHSPROPAGANDALEITUNG / FOLGE 19, 4.–10. MAI 1941
ZENTRALVERLAG DER NSDAP., MÜNCHEN

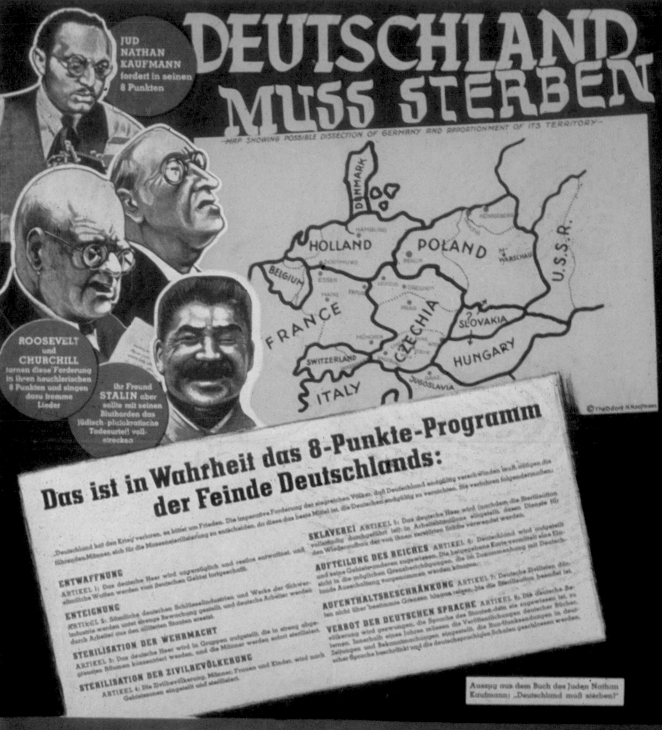

Englands Schuld

Opposite page: This 1941 poster makes use of a book published in the United States titled *Germany Must Perish* (the top of the poster states: "Germany Must Die!"). It advocated the sterilization of the German population and the dismemberment of Germany (the map in the poster is taken from the book and shows how German territory would be distributed among its neighbors). The book was insignificant, but the Nazis presented it as official Allied policy.

Above: "England's Guilt." A poster that tried to cast the British Empire in a negative light, and undermine Britain's self-proclaimed position as the defender of freedom. It makes the point that many African and Asian people in the British Empire had little freedom, a not entirely false accusation. After all, many colonial troops in British military service routinely received inferior rations, lower pay, and discriminatory treatment

Führer. All 10-year-olds into the Hitler Youth." The Nazis viewed the children of today as the soldiers of tomorrow. The Hitler Youth was the most famous youth organization created by the Nazis. There were three others: the League of Young Girls, which covered girls aged 10 to 14; the League of German Girls (from 14 to 18); the German Young People for boys aged 10 to 14; and the Hitler Youth itself, for boys aged 14 to 18. By 1936, when membership of the Hitler Youth was compulsory, there were 5.4 million members of the Nazi youth movement.

the home front as part of the Hitler Youth. As with all Nazi posters, Germans were presented as the finest examples of Aryan stock. The youth in the foreground is wearing the uniform of a Luftwaffe auxiliary, called a *Flakhelfer*. His job was to assist in an antiaircraft battery. By 1943, nearly every flak unit in Germany was manned by Hitler Youth *Flakhelfers*, and by May 1945 over 200,000 *Flakhelfers* were active on all fronts.

Wir ALLE helfen mit!

KRIEGSEINSATZ der HITLERJUGEND

OPPOSITE: These posters were issued in late 1941 in Austria. They were aimed at complainers and those who failed to realize the greatness of life in Nazi Germany. Each poster would hang for two weeks, so the whole campaign ran for three months. Newspapers promoted it, and those attending movie theaters saw slides of the posters before the film began. The goal was to make everyone aware of the two unpleasant central figures in the campaign, and encourage them to behave differently.

1 This poster introduced the two characters: Frau Keppelmeier and Herr Lemperer. The poem runs:

"Frau Keppelmeier, as one can see,
Is deeply troubled as can be.
Herr Lemperer, on the other hand,
Eagerly hears the rumor she tells."

2 Herr Lemperer is not eager to donate to the Nazi Party's charity, the *Winterhilfswerk*, or WHW:

"Herr Lemperer, it's very clear,
Makes his 'sacrifice' so dear.
'Hey,' he mutters, 'I gives ma share!'
Two cents is all that he can spare."

3 Frau Keppelmeier commits the crime (and it was a crime) of listening to British radio:

"At night Frau Keppelmeier turns her dial,
And listens in on London.
She sits there listening to lies,
Happily being led astray."

4 Herr Lemperer, meanwhile, has advice for Hitler's generals:

"Herr Lemperer is a strategist.
The most important thing in any battle
Is to make the right attack, he says.
Any general could learn from him.
One need only listen to him at the pub."

5 Frau Keppelmeier, meanwhile, is having trouble finding the things she needs:

"Frau Keppelmeier is most distressed.
She can't get the right perfume these days.
And our youth, why they're so immature,
They've never heard of perfumed soap!"

6 Herr Lemperer is off to the countryside looking for black market foodstuffs:

"Herr Lemperer, meanwhile, complains so loudly.
The trains, you see, are sometimes late.
In such hard times, how can he then,
Himself punctually fill his sack?"

2

Herr Semperer, das ist ja klar
Auch er bringt hier sein „Opfer" dar.
Meint mürrisch: „Na i gib ja eh!"
Und gibt zwei Pfennig fürs WHW.

3

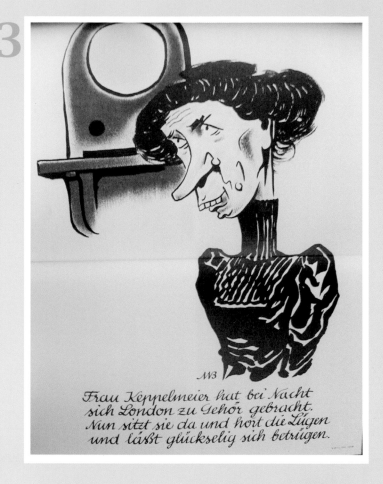

Frau Keppelmeier hat bei Nacht
sich London zu Gehör gebracht.
Nun sitzt sie da und hört die Lügen
und läßt glückselig sich betrügen.

5

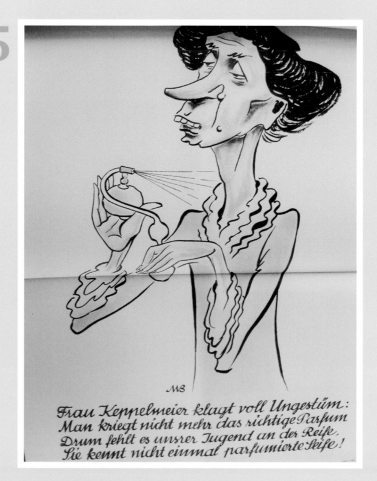

Frau Keppelmeier klagt voll Ungestüm:
Man kriegt nicht mehr das richtige Parfüm
Drum fehlt es unsrer Jugend an der Reife,
Sie kennt nicht einmal parfümierte Seife!

6

Herr Semperer sich sehr beschwert:
Die Eisenbahn unpünktlich fährt.
Wie soll er in so schweren Jahren
In Zukunft pünktlich hamstern fahren?

UNSERE

Luftwaffe

Garanten
deutscher
Wehrkraft !

hand extending from above with a finger pointing accusingly at a Jewish man wearing a top hat and a yellow Star of David on his coat, which is labelled "Jew." Rabid anti-Semitism was a constant theme of Nazi ideology before and during the war. A sub-strand of this was the international Jewish conspiracy against Germany. In 1938 Hitler had said: "We know that they [the Jews] are representatives of an international anti-German movement and we shall treat them all accordingly. They can but lie, defame, and slander, while we know very well that not one of these Jewish agitators would ever join the fight in a war, even though they are the only ones to profit from these wars!"

depicted all the Allied powers as being run by a secret Jewish conspiracy. By the end of 1941 Germany was fighting Britain, the Soviet Union, and the United States. On January 30, 1941, Hitler proclaimed: "I predicted on September 1, 1939, before the German Reichstag—and I am careful to refrain from rash promises—that this war will not end the way the Jews would have it, namely with the extermination of all European and Aryan peoples, but that the result will be the annihilation of the Jewish race." These words would be chillingly prophetic.

Hinter den Feindmächten: der Jude

Der
Einzelne muss und wird
wie immer vergehn, allein
DAS VOLK
MUSS BLEIBEN
ADOLF HITLER

LEFT: "Build Weapons for the Front." This poster was produced in the summer of 1943 when Germany was about to launch its last great offensive on the Eastern Front, at Kursk. Following the defeat at Stalingrad the army had rebuilt its tank arm. In 1943 German industry produced 17,300 tanks and 27,000 artillery pieces. Unfortunately for the Third Reich, the efforts of industry came to nothing, as the army suffered a major defeat at Kursk. Henceforth the Wehrmacht was on the defensive on the Eastern Front, and Germany faced the prospect of losing the war.

BELOW: This Mjölnir poster of 1943 translates as "One Battle, One Will, One Goal: Victory at any Price!" Defeats at the front resulted in a determined effort by the Central Propaganda Office to keep the war effort going. New guidelines stated: "When hanging posters, be sure that their effectiveness is not reduced by other posters. The Central Office for Politically Important Poster Actions has been informed, and instructed to reserve areas for these posters. It is further planned to provide the *Gau* propaganda offices with text banners, small posters, and stickers to post in public transportation and in publicly available offices (police, post offices, ration card offices, economic offices, labor offices, etc.)."

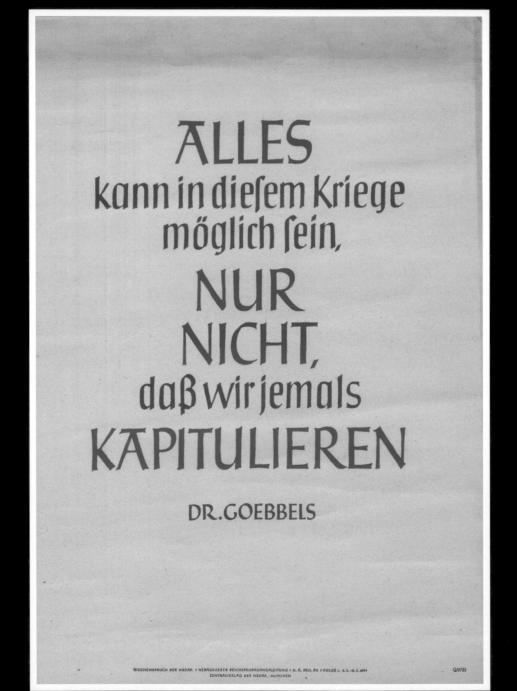

WEHRSCHIESSEN
DES
DEUTSCHEN VOLKES 1944

heading of the poster, but the *Volkssturm* (a sort of National Guard) was a paper tiger. Hitler had decreed that it would contain "all German men aged between 16 and 60 who are capable of bearing arms. It will defend the homeland with all weapons and all means that seem appropriate." But the *Volkssturm* had few weapons, little training, and poor morale.

Nazi eagle holding a wreathed swastika in its talons. In his tunic is the ribbon of the Iron Cross, and behind him is the personal standard of the Führer, signifying the SS's role as Hitler's bodyguard.

BELOW: "You Likewise." A recruiting poster encouraging members of the Hitler Youth to join the 12th SS Panzer Division *Hitlerjugend*. Hitler signed the decree authorizing the formation of the division in April 1943. It was first committed to combat, in June 1944, against the Allies in Normandy. The division contained 18,000 troops, and they fought with Nazi fanaticism as they tried to hold back the Allies. They failed, and by September 1944 the division numbered only 1,500 men.

OPPOSITE PAGE: "United Front Fights Bolshevism." Thousands of Europeans joined the Waffen-SS during the war. A main reason was that they wanted to fight against communism. Indeed, the oath that was sworn by those who served in the foreign legions raised by the Waffen-SS in Western Europe reinforced the myth that they were defending Europe, not just Germany, against the evils of Bolshevik Russia: "I swear by God, this sacred oath, that in the struggle against Bolshevism, I will unconditionally obey the Commander-in-Chief of the Armed Forces, Adolf Hitler, and as a faithful soldier am ready, at any time he may desire, to lay down my life for this oath."

Auch Dir

FELLES FRONT MOT
BOLSJEVISMEN

chapter 4

Italian Posters

World War II was a total disaster for Italy. On June 10, 1940, Benito Mussolini, the fascist leader of the country, had declared war on France and Britain. Both countries had de facto already been defeated by Germany in a Blitzkrieg campaign that had ejected the British Army from the continent and humiliated the French Army. In a speech in Rome Mussolini declared:"An hour marked by destiny is striking in the skies of our Fatherland. The hour of irrevocable decisions. The declaration of war has been sent to the ambassadors of Great Britain and France. We are entering the field of battle against the plutocratic and reactionary democracies of the West, who at every turn have impeded the march, and often threatened the very existence, of the Italian people. People of Italy! Run to your arms and display your tenacity, your courage, and your worth!"

Benito Mussolini

Benito Mussolini (1883—1945), former journalist and fascist dictator of Italy between 1922 to 1943, was obsessed with propaganda. The Italian press, radio, education, and film industry were carefully controlled to manufacture the illusion that Italian fascism was "the doctrine of the twentieth century that was replacing liberalism and democracy," and that Mussolini himself was "a man who was always right and could solve all the problems of politics and economics." The whole media was directed toward building up the cult of the *Duce* (leader). Posters, the press, radio, and cinema were all used to project his image as the omnipotent and indispensable ruler of Italy. By the end of the 1920s, the process of what one could call Mussolini's "image-building" was well under way. The focus of this operation was on Mussolini himself as the sole fascist savior of Italy. By the end of the 1930s, a whole raft of regulations had been established by the Ministry of Popular Culture for the treatment of Mussolini in the media (newspapers, radio, and cinema): his name was always spelt with capital letters in print; newspapers were instructed exactly what to say about him; and he was never to be portrayed dancing, or with priests.

Man of the people

Italian propaganda was very different from German propaganda. Mussolini was portrayed as being "of the people" (his father had been a blacksmith). Fascist Italy was still a poor and economically underdeveloped country, a largely rural and agrarian society. In 1945, for example, over 50 percent of the working population was employed on the land. So Mussolini, stripped to the waist, working in the fields alongside peasants in the "Battle for Grain," the massive national campaign to increase cereals production and reduce dependence on food imports, was a vital propaganda device. This contrasts sharply with Nazi Germany, where posters depicted Hitler in a distant, aloof way. The German Führer, for example, would never be portrayed semi-naked working alongside farm workers.

The first fascist dictator of Europe was naturally obsessed with thoughts of personal glory. He imagined himself Julius Caesar reborn, a genius who would oversee the birth of a "New Roman Empire" in the Mediterranean. That he had no master plan for such a project was of little concern to him.

Italian propaganda promoted the idea of Italian strength. Like Hitler's Thousand Year Reich, Mussolini's Italy was on a path that would lead to glory and aggrandisement. This seemed to be confirmed when Italy overran two weaker countries—Abyssinia in 1936 and Albania in March 1939—conflicts which resulted in Italy being condemned in the international community and pushed Mussolini toward Nazi Germany. Mussolini first referred to a Rome-Berlin Axis in November 1936, and thereafter there was cooperation between the two countries in foreign policy. Both aided the Nationalists in the Spanish Civil War, and it is true to say that Mussolini and Hitler shared a deep affinity with each other as the leaders of populist and revolutionary movements.

Italian resources

In the late 1930s, Mussolini recognized that Italy did not have the resources to participate in a European war. Notwithstanding the claims of Italian propaganda, national income was less than a quarter of that of Britain. Mussolini tried to persuade Hitler not to attack Poland, but the Führer indicated that war was inevitable. *Il Duce* was content to remain neutral when Germany attacked Poland in September 1939, a stance that earned him the contempt of senior Nazis. Hermann Göring remarked that Mussolini was a man who "was yesterday ready to march and is now passive and reticent."

However, by early 1940 Mussolini was jealous of Hitler. He had nothing to compare with the territorial gains made by Germany. In May *Il Duce*'s frustration increased when Hitler struck in the West and routed Britain and France. It appeared that Germany would

BENITO MUSSOLINI
DUCE DEL FASCISMO - FONDATORE DELL'IMPERO

ABOVE: Benito Mussolini, the first fascist dictator of Europe. A man of limited talents but possessed of an enormous ego and thirst for glory. His dream of creating a "New Roman Empire" resulted in a number of disastrous Italian campaigns in World War II, most notably in North Africa and Greece in 1940. Hitler's conquests in the same year only made him more desperate to win battlefield glory.

win the war, and that Italy would receive pickings from the French Empire (in accordance with an understanding between the two dictators made before the war). To earn the right to these spoils, Mussolini decided that he must fight France—he declared war on June 10, 1940.

Balkan disaster

Unfortunately for Mussolini, in the subsequent armistice between France and Germany his claim to French overseas territory was largely ignored. Mussolini thus needed some glory to maintain his prestige abroad and rally support at home. In October 1940, therefore, he ordered an attack on Greece from the Italian colony of Albania. However, after initial Italian gains the Greeks forced the Italian Army back onto Albanian soil. By December 1940 there was stalemate on the Greek Front. To add insult to injury, the Italian fleet, at anchor at Taranto in southern Italy, was badly damaged by a British torpedo attack in mid-November. This action tilted the balance of naval power in the Mediterranean decisively toward the British.

By this date the Italian Army in North Africa had also suffered a crushing defeat at the hands of the British. Despite Italian posters proclaiming that the army was on the march to Egypt, save for the arrival of Erwin Rommel in February 1941 Italian forces might have been ejected from North Africa altogether.

Italian propaganda always talked of strength, but the reality was that there was no militaristic culture in Italy. The prestige of the army in Italy itself was not especially high, and it was the same with the navy. A major problem for Mussolini was that the armed forces were not particularly attractive to well-educated and technically skilled men, not that an industrially under-developed Italy possessed these in great numbers. The officer corps, therefore, was of a low caliber. The situation was made worse by the fact that much of the army's weapons and equipment were obsolete.

Mussolini believed that he could win fresh laurels for Italian arms by taking part in Hitler's attack on the Soviet Union in June 1941. He was convinced he would gain the prestige that he longed for, and Italy would share in the spoils of war. He thus joined the war against Russia and committed a force of 60,000 men to the struggle, known as the *Corp di Spedizione Italiano* (CSI—Italian Expeditionary Corps in Russia).

In July 1941, the supposedly motorized CSI followed the German Army through the Ukraine, mainly on foot. Morale was high at the prospect of an easy campaign, though, and the Germans were impressed with their Italian allies. Unfortunately this initial euphoria soon disappeared. Inadequate leadership,

armor, and transportation, plus shortages of artillery and antitank weapons, revealed the corps to be ill-equipped for the campaign. Undeterred, in March 1942 Mussolini sent more reinforcements to Russia. The 227,000 Italians on the Eastern Front became the Italian Eighth Army. In August 1942, it was guarding the Don Front north of Stalingrad with German liaison officers and formations attached to ensure its reliability. Although a Russian attack had been expected, the Italians were unable to resist the massive armored thrust that was hurled against them on December 11, 1942. II and XXXV Corps crumbled almost immediately, leaving the Alpine Corps stranded and resulting in a huge gap in the Don defenses. The lack of antitank guns and medium tanks was keenly felt in this rout. The Italians were left to fend for themselves during their retreat, in which they were harassed continually by the Red Army. In January 1943, the survivors regrouped in the Ukraine but the Italian Eighth Army had ceased to exist. The disillusioned Germans sent the survivors back to Italy.

In May 1943 the Axis war effort in North Africa came to an end, with 250,000 Germans and Italians going into Allied captivity. The war, which had never been popular among the Italian populace, was about to come to the homeland. In early July 1943, the Allies invaded Sicily, and on July 25 a vote of no confidence was passed on *Il Duce* by the Fascist Grand Council. He was toppled from power, as was the Fascist Party itself, which was dissolved. Control of the government passed to King Victor Emmanuel III and control of the army to Marshal Badoglio. Mussolini's 20-year-old dictatorship was at an end. The Italians wanted to quit the war and Badoglio entered into secret negotiations with the Allies, but the Germans moved quickly to occupy Italy. The Allies invaded Italy on September 3, 1943, but by then the Germans were firmly in control of the country and had disarmed the Italian Army.

The fascist rump state

A virtual civil war had broken out in Italy after Mussolini's fall and Italy's exit from the Axis camp. Some of the Italian forces actively resisted the Germans and were defeated and made prisoner, others deserted to swell the ranks of the resistance, but a few remained loyal to fascism and Mussolini. The Germans were anxious to utilize the pro-fascist elements in the struggle against the now greatly augmented resistance. Above all, they were determined to keep open the vital lines of communication between Austria and northern Italy. Mussolini was rescued from captivity by German special forces, and in September 1943 he established

the Fascist Republican Party as the ruling party of the Italian Social Republic. Mussolini's republic cannot be considered anything but a puppet state of the greater German Reich. Four infantry divisions were formed and trained in Germany: the *Italia*, *Littorio*, *San Marco*, and *Monterosa* Divisions. These and other units were under German control.

The failure of Italian fascism

The "Charter of Verona" of the Italian Social Republic echoed the propaganda of earlier periods. It stated: "The essential goal of the foreign policy of the Republic must be the unity, independence, and territorial integrity of the Fatherland within its maritime and Alpine frontiers constituted by nature, blood sacrifice, and history."

The Social Republic was merely a German puppet state, though, with little support among the Italian population. Italians had not only been dragged into German battles in North Africa, but had then lived under German occupation and endured two long years of war as the Allies fought their way north in the face of a dogged Wehrmacht defense. Italian towns and cities had been bombed and fought over, and the Germans had taken savage reprisals against those they suspected of being partisans. Small wonder, then, that the people took revenge on Mussolini and his mistress after they had been killed by partisans in April 1945. Their bodies were hung up in Milan's Piazalle Loreto in front of cheering crowds.

Eight days before he was shot, Mussolini gave an interview with a journalist. He talked fondly of Hitler and also of German wonder weapons that would turn the tide of the war. But in truth he was still living in the fantasy world he had inhabited since the outbreak of World War II: "The victory of the so-called Allied Powers will give to the world only an ephemeral and illusory peace," and that "history will vindicate me." He was wrong on both counts.

Opposite page: "Every day the battlefield nears its destination." An Italian boast that the army was heading toward Egypt following the Italian offensive from Libya launched in September 1940. In reality, the Italians advanced 65 miles (104 km) and then stopped. In December 1940, the British counterattacked and routed the Italians in a humiliating defeat. For the Italian Army, it was a foretaste of the military disasters that were to come in the war.

MATRUH
SSANDRIA
SUEZ

OGNI GIORNO DI BATTAGLIA
CI AVVICINA ALLA META

...se non ci fosse stata la Marcia su Roma non ci sarebbe oggi la marcia su Mosca...

MOSCA-1941
MADRID-1936
ROMA-1922

FEDERAZIONE DEI FASCI DI COMBATTIMENTO DI MILANO
VENTENNALE

LA DONNA ITALIANA COLLE SUE RINUNCE E COI SUOI SACRIFICI, MARCIA INSIEME AI COMBATTENTI.

Opposite page: "Without the March on Rome. No March on Moscow." A poster heralding Italian participation in Operation Barbarossa, linking it to Mussolini's March on Rome in 1922 and the Nationalist victory at Madrid in 1936. In fact, the "March" was a myth created by the fascists for propaganda purposes. Mussolini was asked to form a government before the march began. In this poster, an Italian fascist Blackshirt is attacking the Russian bear. The Italian forces that took part in Barbarossa were woefully short of antitank guns, tanks, and

Above: "The Italian Woman, by her renunciations and her sacrifices, marches along with the fighting men." In Italy there was little enthusiasm for the war among the general population. Even among government circles the conflict was viewed with dread. In June 1940, the foreign minister, Count Ciano, expressed his doubts: "I am sad, very sad. May God help Italy!"

BELOW: "Conquer! For the New World Order." A poster emphasizing the Axis alliance between Japan, Italy, and Germany. To Mussolini, Japan was a Far Eastern version of Italy itself. In December 1942 he gave a speech in Rome, stating: "That Japan, which was a country as poor as we, has become, within a few months, if not the first in wealth among the nations of the world, certainly one of the first. Well, it must be recognized that this is just; that it is the reward of Japan's virtue."

OPPOSITE PAGE: "Young fascists—heroes of Bir-el-Gobi." This poster is one of the most accurate depictions of the North African war produced by the Italians in World War II, though they did not realize it at the time. It is supposed to portray Italian martial prowess, but in fact it is a summary of the state of the Italian Army while fighting the British in North Africa. In June 1940, Marshal Italo Balbo, Governor of Libya, told the Italian General Staff: "We don't have armored cars, the antitank guns are usually old and noneffective, the new ones lack adequate ammunition. Thus the combat becomes a sort of meat-against-iron-fighting."

GIOVANI FASCISTI
EROI DI BIR-EL-GOBI

BOERI · INDIANI · EGIZIANI · ARABI · IRLANDE/I ·

Per la Gran Bretagna tutte le razze e tutti i popoli sono uguali.

ACTA - Milano - Escule da bollo · Stab. Grafico Ripalta - Milano

I DELITTI INUMANI DEI "GANGSTERS PILOTI" RADIANO
PER SEMPRE GLI STATI UNITI DAL CONSORZIO CIVILE

OPPOSITE PAGE: "The English treat all races equally." Axis propaganda frequently attacked Allied nations, especially Britain and France, for their treatment of non-Europeans in their respective empires. This was not out of concern for Asian or African peoples; rather, it was to highlight Allied hypocrisy. The Allies were seemingly fighting for equality and freedom, rights that they were denying their own colonial subjects. On another level, posters such as this were subconscious expressions of annoyance that Italy was being denied her own overseas possessions and thus her "place in the sun."

ABOVE: "The Inhuman Crimes of Gangster Pilots Always Receive Radioed Orders Directly From the United States Civil Government." This poster is an attempt to discourage the Italian people from assisting American aviators by trying to equate American pilots with gangsters. It was a tactic that failed: by 1943, when this poster was produced, the Italian people hated the Germans much more than they did the Allies.

BELOW: "Italian Workers! The 'liberators' are already thinking about the future of your children." The theme of the barbarous foe was a common one in Axis propaganda. Except with regard to Nazi fears of what the Red Army would do once on German soil, it was mostly fantasy. In fact, many Italians welcomed the Allies when they invaded the mainland in September 1943. Italians felt that their country had been engaged in an illegal and aggressive conflict, and as the war progressed with great loss of life, they became increasingly disenchanted.

OPPOSITE PAGE: A poster calling for Italians to join the Organization Todt, the Nazi organization that was responsible for building military factories and fortifications throughout the Third Reich. It employed many foreign workers, prisoners of war, and concentration camp inmates. In reality, thousands of Italians were forced to work for the organization when the Germans occupied the country, helping to build fortifications such as the Gustav Line in central Italy.

Italiani!
date la vostra opera
all'ORGANIZZAZIONE TODT
per lavori in
Italia

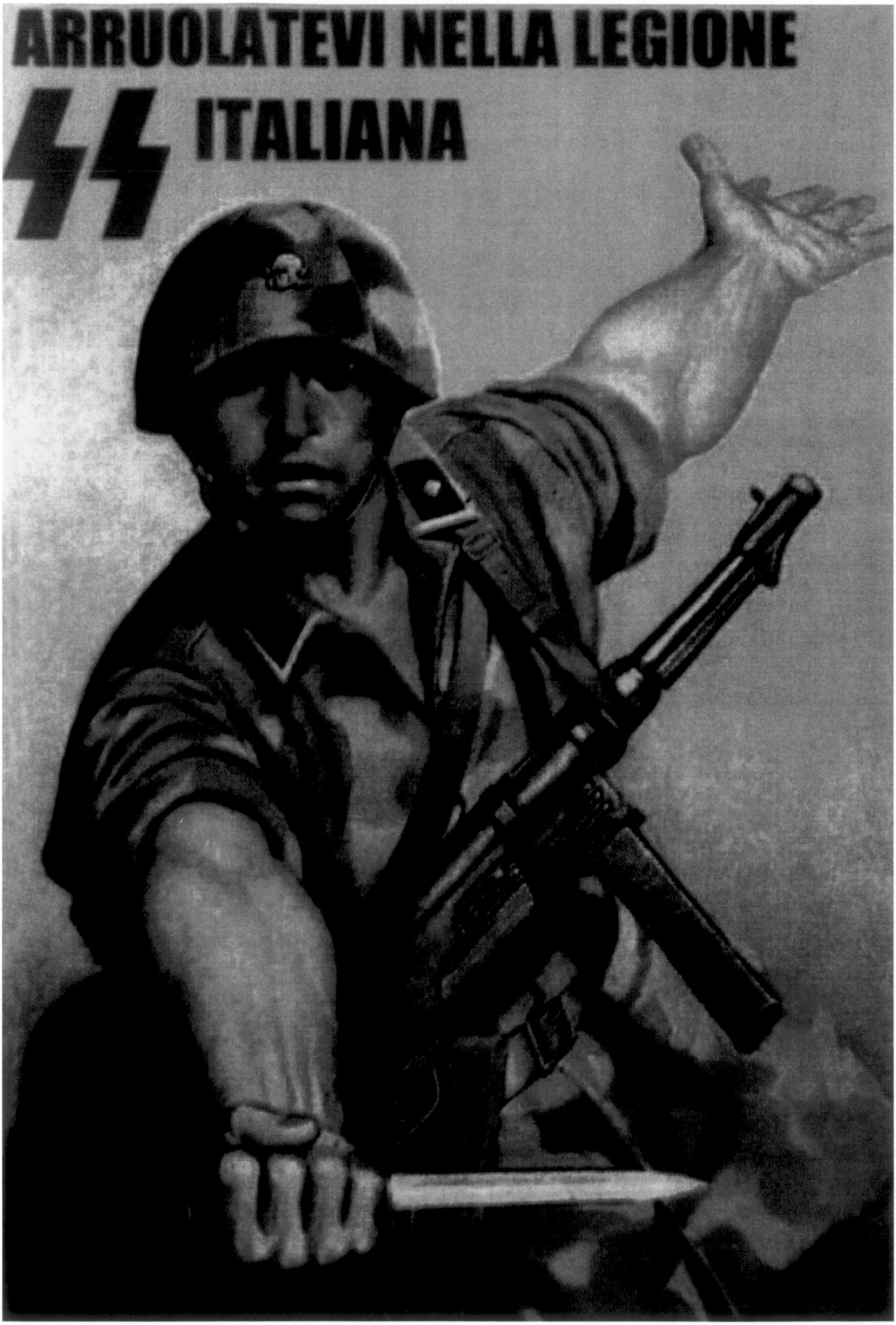
ARRUOLATEVI NELLA LEGIONE
SS ITALIANA

IMPEDISCI CHE QUESTO DELITTO SI COMPIA

Vota
BLOCCO NAZIONALE
nè reazione nè rivoluzione

OPPOSITE PAGE: A Waffen-SS recruiting poster aimed at Italians. The recruiting drive had some success. The 29th Grenadier Division of the Italian SS was composed of 15,000 Italian recruits who volunteered for service with the Waffen-SS. In addition, in September 1943 to the end of February 1944, a separate SS battalion was formed at the SS Heidelager Training Center at Debica, Poland. The volunteers came from the Italian 31st Tank Battalion of the *Lombardia* Division and the élite Alpine *Julia* Division. The formation, which had 20 officers and 571 men, was referred to as the SS Battalion *Debica*.

ABOVE: A poster of the National Bloc, one of the parties that took part in the Italian elections held in 1948. By this time the Cold War between the West and the USSR was raging and Italy became one of the battlegrounds between communism and democracy. The National Bloc (*Blocco Nazionale*) was a political coalition of liberals and conservatives. The poster plays on the fears of a communist takeover of Italy, which the Bloc believed would lead to the death of Italian freedom. The communists were not voted into power, but neither was the National Bloc. As a result, the Bloc disappeared soon after.

Japanese Posters

j apanese propaganda before and during World War II was directed toward assisting Japan become a great power in Asia. This involved carrying out an anti-Western campaign in the media (since Western colonial powers controlled lands that Tokyo coveted for the Empire of the Sun), and convincing the indigenous peoples of Southeast Asia that they would benefit more under Japanese influence rather than under European rule. Allied to this general expansionist propaganda, there was also a sense of grievance.

Japanese resentment

Despite siding with the Allies in World War I, Japan felt, with some justification, that its status in the world was not confirmed. Tokyo had gained some Pacific colonies in the Allied territorial share out, but was also forced to relinquish Chinese regions conquered during the Russo-Japanese War of 1904–1905. In Japanese eyes, insult was added to injury in 1922 when the Washington Naval Treaty limited the size of the Japanese Navy to below that of the U.S. and British fleets, despite the fact that the quality and quantity of Japanese shipping could match and even exceed Allied fleets in the Pacific.

To a people with an extremely high concept of respect, this "loss of face" was stinging, particularly amongst the leaders of the Japanese Army, whose philosophy retained strong elements of anti-Westernism. To make matters worse, the Japanese were aware that their entire industrial revolution was dependent upon U.S. and colonial imports. Almost every vital domestic and industrial product, including food, rubber, and most metals, had to be imported, and the United States supplied around 60 percent of Japanese oil. This dependence on the outside world rubbed salt into the Japanese wound, and many felt that Japan had been relegated to a second-class nation within its own geographical region of influence.

War in China

The Japanese solution to its problem was expansion, aiming to achieve self-sufficiency through conquering territories which could provide plentiful raw materials and food stocks. It first looked toward its neighbor, China. In 1931 Japan invaded and occupied Manchuria, a country rich in mineral resources, and in 1937 it invaded China itself. The war between China and Japan turned into a hugely violent and costly eight-year conflict, in which the Japanese Army committed many atrocities.

The war in China may have been seen as naked aggression in Western eyes, but in Japan it was portrayed as virtuous. Japanese propaganda was highly critical of the interference of white Western countries in Asia, specifically the French in Indochina, the British in Hong Kong and Malaysia, and the United States in the Philippines.

Japanese propaganda in the interwar period criticized Western nations for their colonies in India and Southeast Asia. White Westerners were portrayed as rich, arrogant colonists who oppressed indigenous peoples and lived off them. In government pamphlets Japanese soldiers were told that "money squeezed from the blood of Asians maintains these small white minorities in their luxurious mode of life." To make matters worse, the Western nations were stealing the wealth of Asian nations in Japan's own backyard. It was therefore Japan's duty to free them from the grip of foreign colonialism. This theme had begun in the early 1930s. In January 1933, the Great Asiatic Association was founded by among others future prime minister Prince Fuminaro Konoye. Other association members included Admiral Nobumasa Suetsugu, later minister of foreign affairs, Minister of Foreign Affairs Koki Hirota, and General Iwane Matsui, later commander-in-chief in China. The association called attention to the "pitiable condition of the Asiatics in countries under white rule." The association advocated that "Hegemony in Asia" should be Japan's official policy. This "Asia for the Asiatics" lobby was accompanied by an intensive press campaign, which in the beginning was directed mainly at Britain as the exponent of so-called Western Imperialism. However, it was later aimed at all Western peoples.

World War II

Japanese propaganda's constant message was that white Westerners were evil and greedy. They were also immoral, as illustrated during World War II by their attacks against Pacific islands and later against Japan itself. The United States was criticized for its treatment of racial minorities and immigrants, pointing to the internment of tens of thousands of Japanese-Americans in camps in the USA.

When World War II broke out in Europe in September 1939, Tokyo saw an opportunity to increase Japanese influence and power in Southeast Asia. On September 27, 1940, with war already raging across Europe, Japan signed the Tripartite Pact with Germany and Italy. The Tripartite Pact committed the

ABOVE: "Rise of Asia." This poster portrays Japan as the savior of Asia, throwing off the shackles of white Western imperialism. It displays several themes common to Japanese propaganda: the weakness of the United States (note the American flag lying trampled on the ground), the strength of the Japanese, and the Japanese soldier ridding Asia of Western forces.

signatories to defend the other countries if they were attacked by any nation other than China or countries already involved in the European conflict. This aligned Japan with the Axis.

In September 1940, Japanese expansion proceeded when, at the invitation of the French, Japanese troops entered northern French Indochina. The Indochina acquisition gave Japan tremendous logistical strength for its war against China and numerous coastal bases to prosecute a naval campaign throughout Southeast Asia. By this time, Japan had already formulated a clear imperialist outlook, looking to establish what it called the "Greater East Asia Co-Prosperity Sphere." This envisaged an East Asia free of colonial influence and united under Japanese hegemony. Japan hoped that the Co-Prosperity Sphere would lead many colonial Asian countries to work, violently or otherwise, toward their independence from British, Dutch, and U.S. influence.

The "good parent"

In 1942, during World War II, the Japanese Government published a booklet entitled *The Greater East Asia War and Ourselves*. It described how the relationship between Asian countries would be like that of a "branch family." It stated: "America, England, Holland, and others, by military force, were suppressing and doing bad things like this to us of Greater East Asia. By our hand, Japan restored Greater East Asia and rose to our feet. And, the strong Japanese expelled the enemy from Greater East Asia. Currently, in Manchuria, everyone has begun combining their power and work. Japan and China formed an alliance. The Philippines and Burma became independent. Thailand grew larger. The people of Java, Malay, and others, too, will, by important duties, come together to work. India, too, has driven out England. From now, we will make the countries of Greater East Asia friendly to one another. We of Greater East Asia will combine our power and bring about the destruction of America, England, and others."

The message pumped out by Tokyo was that Japan was like a good parent who was concerned only with the general wellbeing of Asian countries. These are the words of Japanese Foreign Minister Hirota: "It is hardly necessary to say that the basic policy of the Japanese Government aims at the stabilization of East Asia through conciliation and cooperation between Japan, Manchukuo, and China for their common prosperity and wellbeing. Since, however, China, ignoring our true motive, has mobilized her vast armies against us, we can only counter her step by force of

arms." Like naughty children, the countries of Asia did not know what was good for them. They therefore sometimes had to be punished. But always Japan was acting in their best interests; indeed, Japan failed to recognize any wrongdoings it may have committed against other countries at all.

The reality of Japanese propaganda

In posters, Japanese soldiers were invariably portrayed as strong and determined, battling to free Asia of white Western enslavers, to throw off the chains that enslaved the native peoples. Of course the Japanese wanted to rule Southeast Asia in place of the West. However, they would do so as part of a program of ethnic unity. This was the Japanese concept of *Hakko Ichiu*, or "eight corners under one roof." In this the Japanese were pandering to the idea of a common Asian race and that there should be ethnic unity under the Japanese "roof." As such, Japanese propaganda could not insult their "brethren" in the same way that it could attack white Westerners. An example of this train of thought is the attitude toward the Koreans, whom the Japanese often described in demeaning and racist language. But at the same time, the Japanese felt a parental duty toward the Koreans, believing them to be redeemable. This idea was expanded to other Southeast Asian peoples. After all; the Japanese wanted the populations of the region to believe in Japan's Co-Prosperity Sphere and take an active part in it, as well as aiding the Japanese in defeating the Western colonial powers. Persuading the Chinese, Koreans, and Southeast Asians that a unified Asia under Japanese leadership was good would be impossible if these groups were portrayed in Japanese posters and booklets as being inferior.

Unfortunately, there were far too many atrocities carried out by Japanese troops to win over the populations of occupied areas. The rape of Nanking during the Sino-Japanese War of 1937–1945 stands as one of the most shameful and controversial incidents in Japanese history. An estimated 200–300,000 Chinese prisoners and civilians were systematically slaughtered in a month-long orgy of bloodletting by Japanese soldiers. The atrocity was the logical outcome of three factors. First, total obedience to the emperor and to the military commanders in the theater (testimony from commanding officers shows that the officer class emphatically embraced the genocide). Second, the mental instability resulting from prolonged combat and separation from home. Third, the contemporary Japanese racism toward other Asian countries, the Chinese being looked on as subhuman in the same way

that the Nazis viewed the Slavs of Eastern Europe and the Soviet Union.

Nanking was not the only location of Japanese atrocities during the Sino-Japanese War. One soldier, Masayo Enomoto, recorded that looting, rape, and murder were common procedures throughout the Chinese campaigns. He confesses to the group rape and murder of women in Chinese villages and even, when rape became a bore, outright torture (he confessed to dousing a young woman with petrol and setting her on fire simply as a form of entertainment). Revealingly, Enomoto admits no sense of guilt because of his total belief in the justice of fighting for the emperor. It would appear to be a sad fact that much of the cause of the Nanking atrocities was the age-old brutalization of soldiers by war and racial indoctrination, combined with the excesses people are capable of when in positions of absolute power.

The notion of purity

Japanese propaganda during World War II also sought to reinforce the image of the Japanese soldier and nation as being pure. Whereas Japan's foes were portrayed as being corrupt and immoral, propaganda told the Japanese that they were racially and spiritually pure. This being the case, the Japanese were bound to triumph over immoral and "impure" enemies, in much the same way that German propaganda spoke of the certainly of victory over "subhuman" enemies. This message undoubtedly boosted Japanese morale, even when Japan's cities were being flattened by American bombers in 1944 and 1945 and Japan was obviously losing the war. The thing that held the Japanese together was their purity, from which came their pride and strength as a nation. These attributes meant they could endure any hardships the enemy could inflict on them. The deaths of over 600,000 Japanese civilians during World War II bears witness to this outlook.

OPPOSITE PAGE: A poster for the 1940 film *The Story of Tank Commander Nishizoemi*. Commissioned by the Ministry of War, in the film the main character sacrifices his life for his men in battle during the war in China. For his sacrifice he is posthumously honored with the title of *gunshin*, or "military god." The film embodies the notion of self-sacrifice, the giving up of oneself for the greater good. It was based on the life of an actual Japanese officer.

佐野部隊長遖らざる大野挺身隊と訣別す　　　　　　　　　　　　田村孝之介筆

x

Opposite page: This poster attacks the British and Americans and encourages the Filipinos to throw off their imperial yoke and join the Co-Prosperity Sphere. During the war, Japanese propaganda had the task of not only addressing the home front but also persuading other Asian countries that Tokyo's rule was beneficial (after first conquering said countries). Without the support of other Asian countries, the Co-Prosperity Sphere would fail. Japanese soldiers were always portrayed in posters with bayonets fixed—reflecting the army's doctrine of mounting bayonet charges whenever possible.

Above: "Accepting an Allied Surrender." A simple poster but one that had a powerful psychological message. Japanese soldiers were highly trained and disciplined, and indoctrinated in a military culture that demanded the highest sacrifices in battle. Obedience to the emperor was everything, and to retreat or be taken prisoner were acts of profound dishonor. To surrender was a disgrace, the action of someone who was weak, impure, and immoral. The implication here is that Allied soldiers are weak and immoral, reflecting the cultures of the states they serve.

BELOW: "Keep Your Lips Silent!" A Japanese version of the "careless talk costs lives" theme. Internal security was rigidly enforced in Japan. Factory police (*kempei*) were present in every war plant, and police agent provocateurs combated defeatism by deliberately making comments about the futility of the war, or corruption on the home front. Any who agreed were ruthlessly punished.

OPPOSITE PAGE: "Buy Japanese War Bonds." War production in Japan was a dismal failure, with little attempt to mass-produce anything. In 1941, for example, most of the army's trucks were imported American models, for which the supply of spare parts dried up after the attack on Pearl Harbor in December 1941.

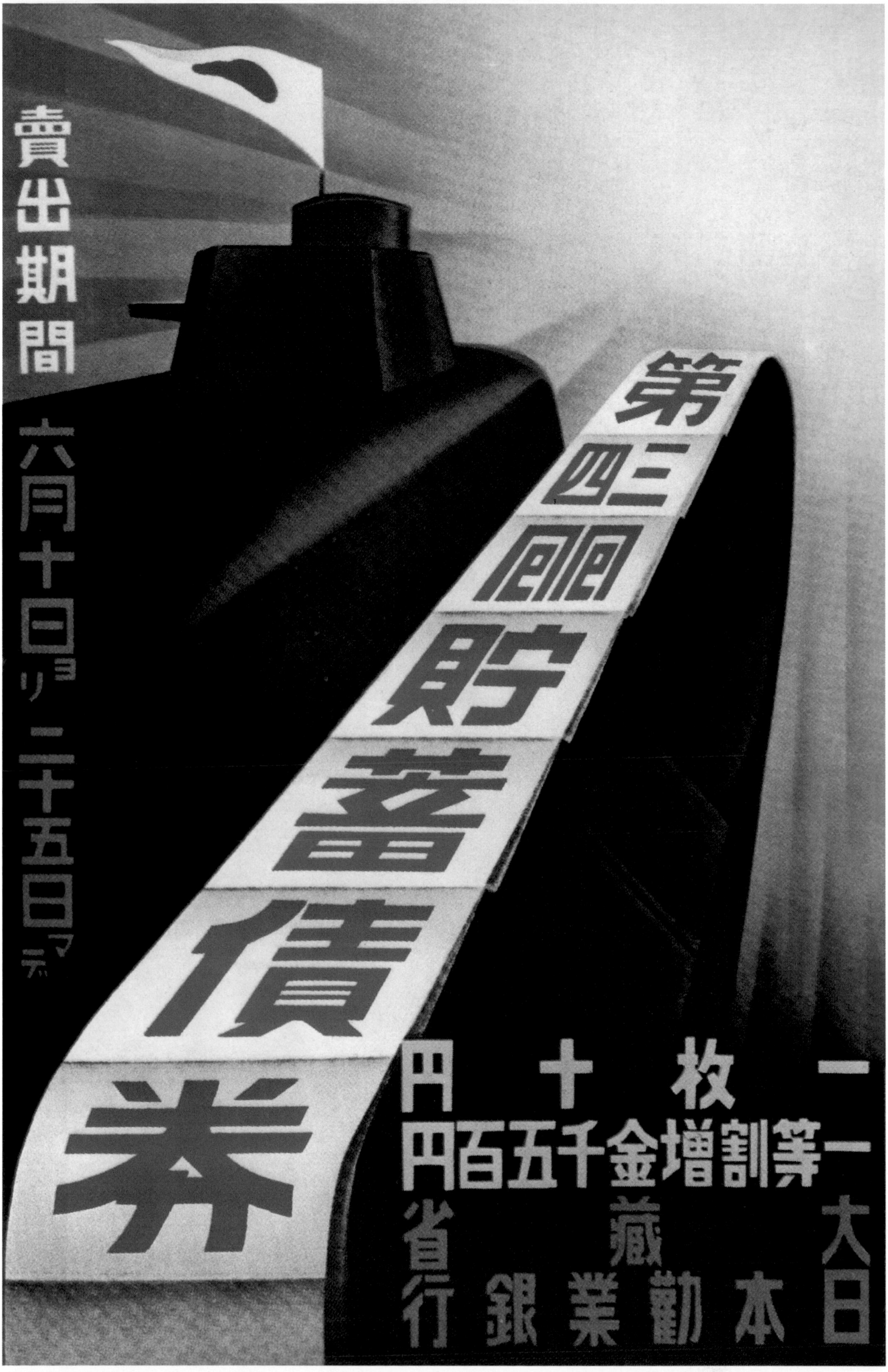
賣出期間
六月十日ヨリ二十五日マデ
第四回貯蓄債券
一枚十円
一等割増金千五百円
大藏省
日本勸業銀行

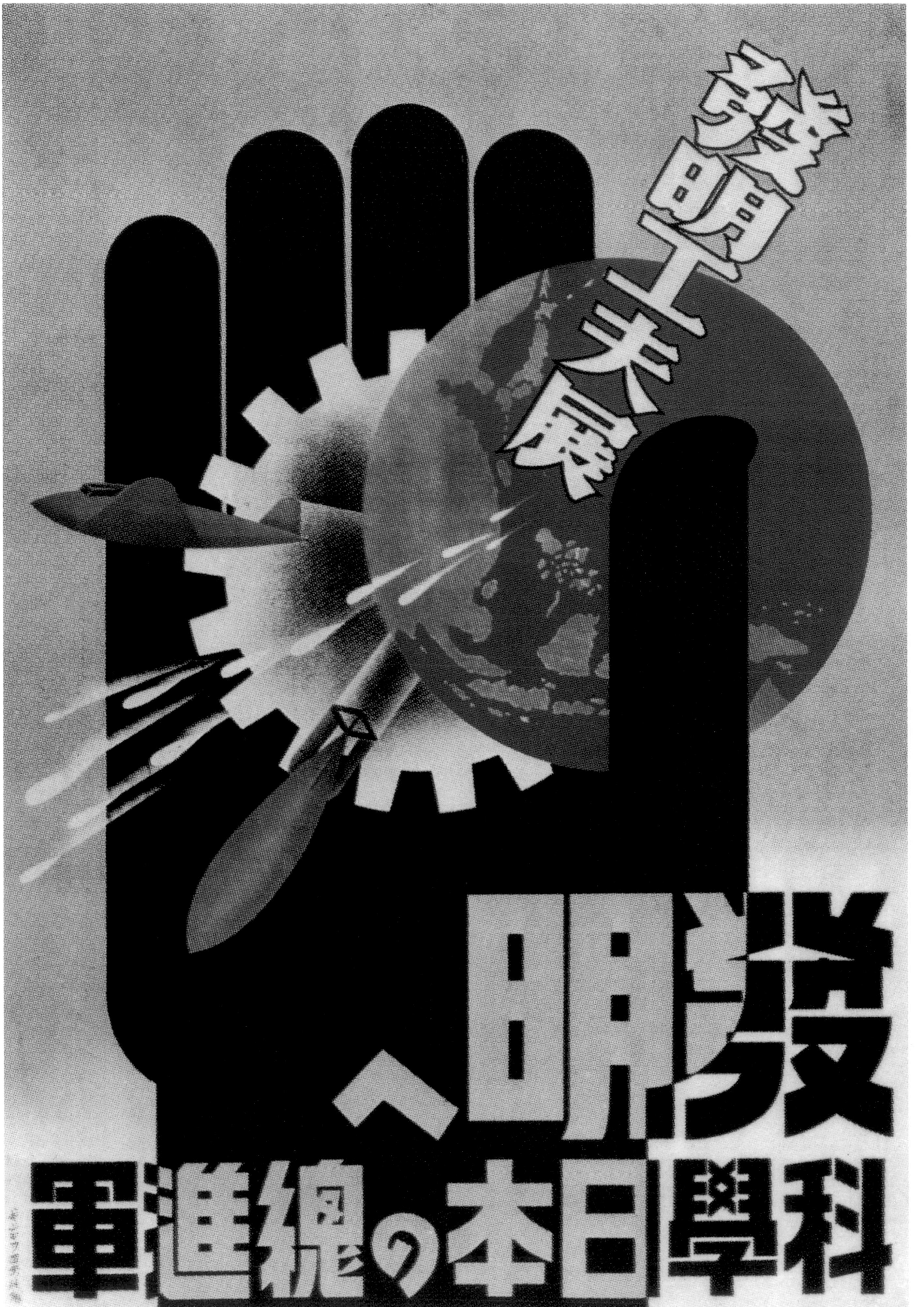
發明工夫展
發明へ
科學日本の總進軍

盧溝橋

田村孝之介筆

OPPOSITE PAGE: "For a scientific Japan." This poster is for an "exhibition of inventions to produce more weapons for war." In reality, Japanese efforts to produce modern weapons were inadequate at best. For example, the production of tanks declined from 1,100 in 1942 to 400 in 1944 and only 142 in 1945. Of the tanks that were produced, most were of the light or medium variety. And as the army had few tanks of its own, it saw little reason to develop antitank weapons. Thus when the Japanese came up against U.S. Sherman tanks in the Pacific, they were forced to resort to using hollowed-out coconut shells filled with explosives as antitank weapons.

ABOVE: "Warriors Rush Into Battle." The celebration of the virtues of offensive action in general was a central theme of Japanese propaganda. Military service was ranked as the highest social duty, and the best and brightest officers were always at the front on the battlefield. Allied to this were deeply held religious beliefs among the Japanese. The emperor had a divine status in the people's eyes, and to die in battle for him was to die a holy death.

Russian Posters

f or the Soviet people, World War II was a remorseless life-and-death struggle against a merciless enemy whose goal was nothing less than the enslavement of the whole population. As such, Soviet propaganda was able to claim the moral high ground in the war, notwithstanding the dreadful crimes of Stalin's regime during the 1930s, in which millions of Russians died, and the fact that the USSR had signed a non-aggression pact with Germany in 1939. Propaganda was supervised by the Directorate of Propaganda and Agitation of the Central Committee under A.S. Shcherbakov, and administered by the Soviet Information Bureau. In the first two years of the war the Soviet Union was on the defensive. Thus the propagandists responded with gusto to rally the people against the Nazi invader. Two days after the Germans attacked, the poster "We will mercilessly destroy" appeared on the streets of Moscow. It showed a caricature of Hitler with a revolver, his head breaking through the torn Soviet-German Non-Aggression Pact of 1939, only to be faced by a determined Red Army soldier whose bayonet pointed at his head (this poster first appeared on June 24, 1941).

The German threat

Relations between Germany and the Soviet Union deteriorated following Adolf Hitler's accession to power in 1933, and Moscow was convinced that Germany would embark on territorial conquest in Eastern Europe. The Soviet Union was faced with a potentially hostile Germany in the west and an anti-communist Japan in the east. Thus Stalin was forced to seek allies in an effort to protect the Soviet Union from aggression, or at least share the burden of any conflict with an aggressor.

He thus looked to the West, specifically Britain and France, as alliance partners to preserve the balance of power in Europe. However, this should not be interpreted as anything more than *realpolitik* on Moscow's part (or indeed on the Western side). Stalin was a pragmatist, and at the end of the day it mattered little to him if he concluded a treaty with Western imperialist powers or fascist states as long as his interests were served. He may have distrusted Nazi Germany, but the same was also true of Britain and France (he called the latter "the most aggressive and most militarist" of the Western states). Nevertheless, he made efforts to mend fences with the West, joining the League of Nations in 1934 and ordering communist parties abroad to abandon the revolutionary struggle. He thus abandoned the USSR's isolationism and embarked on a policy of collective security.

Western prevarication

The first real test came in the summer of 1938 when Germany threatened Czechoslovakia. Both France and the Soviet Union were treaty bound to come her aid if she was attacked, and Stalin for his part was prepared to honor his commitments. The subsequent Munich Agreement saved Europe from war but intensified Stalin's mistrust of the West. The USSR was not invited to participate in the Munich talks in September 1938. When Germany occupied the rest of Czechoslovakia in March 1939, Stalin made a fresh, albeit reluctant, effort to form a collective security alliance with Britain and France. On April 17, 1939, the USSR offered both countries an alliance that would guarantee the integrity of every state from the Mediterranean to the Baltic. But Britain and France prevaricated. Britain did not reply until May 25, agreeing not to the treaty but the opening of preliminary discussions, and not until August 12 did French and British low-level negotiators arrive in Moscow for talks. It became clear to Stalin that Britain and France were very reluctant allies. The search for collective security was over, and the road was clear for a mutually beneficial non-aggression pact between Germany and the USSR. Despite the huge gulf in ideology, German Foreign Minister Joachim von Ribbentrop flew to the Soviet Union in August, and signed an agreement with his recently appointed opposite number, Vyacheslav Molotov, on August 24. The Ribbentrop-Molotov Pact contained a 10-year non-aggression agreement, while other clauses specified the division of Poland between the two countries. Stalin was given a free hand in Finland, the Baltic States of Estonia, Latvia, and Lithuania, and Bessarabia (in Romania). Stalin was buying time and land as a buffer against Germany. For his part, Hitler had a secure eastern border so he could campaign freely in Western Europe.

The defense of Mother Russia

"Defend Mother Russia" was the cry that Stalin used to rally the Russian people in June 1941. When Germany invaded the Soviet Union in June 1941, Stalin was initially stunned, but quickly recovered to direct the war effort. Abandoning the concept of a defense of international communism, the wily dictator instead issued a call to arms in the name of Russian nationalism (indeed, in Soviet eyes the conflict became The Great Patriotic War). Less than a week after the

ABOVE: "The result of fascist culture." This poster by Pavel Petrovich Sokolov-Skalia (1899–1961) shows three scenes, in each of which Hitler is attempting to destroy Russian culture. The Russian cultural icons depicted are, from top to bottom: Leo Tolstoy, Mikhail Vasilyevich Lomonosov, and Peter the Great. In Soviet posters Adolf Hitler was invariably portrayed as a beast with blood-stained limbs and an insatiable appetite for gore.

German attack the State Printing Works had produced a poster with the title "The Motherland is calling You!" It was an inspired illustration. A steely faced elder mother in a shawl calls out to the observer. She is dressed in simple attire, thus enabling the vast majority of Russians to identify with her. In her hand she holds the oath of loyalty to the Red Army soldier. The poster was very popular throughout the Soviet Union, millions of copies being printed, and in all the main languages of the USSR.

In a rousing speech he gave in Moscow's Red Square in November 1941, when German panzers were fast approaching the city, Stalin invoked the memory of past Russian heroes to inspire resistance against the Nazi invader: "The war you are waging is a war of liberation, a just war. Let the heroic images of our great ancestors—Alexander Nevsky, Dmitri Donskoi, Kusma Minin, Dmitri Pozharsky, Alexander Suvorov, Mikhail Kutuzov—inspire you in this war! Long live our glorious Motherland, her freedom and her independence!"

Stalin's iron rule

A year later the Soviet people were still fighting, but had suffered enormous losses. The 1942 poster "Red Army soldier, Save Us!" epitomizes this suffering. A young mother with a child in her arms and hate in her eyes is being threatened by a Nazi bayonet. The caption in red appears to have been written by the blood dripping from the bayonet. Ironically, Stalin was largely indifferent to Soviet losses, once stating: "One death is a tragedy, one million is a statistic." When his beloved wife Ekaterina died of typhus in 1908 he reportedly said, "and with her died my last warm feelings for all human beings." His brutality was legendary: in the 1930s his efforts at collectivization resulted in the deaths of up to 10 million peasants through starvation; the Great Purge of the Red Army between 1937 and 1941 resulted in the deaths of 35,000 officers and men executed on suspicion of being "counter-revolutionaries," although they were in fact killed because in Stalin's eyes they represented a potential threat to his rule.

German forces perpetuated atrocities on a massive scale during the invasion of the USSR, and Soviet propaganda responded in kind, preaching hatred toward the enemy. German forces were presented as bestial and immoral. Like American propaganda toward the Japanese, Soviet posters created a dehumanized image of the Germans. They were "fascist beasts" fit only to be slaughtered. Berlin itself was described as the "lair of the fascist beast."

As with the enemy, no mercy was shown toward Soviet citizens who did not show a total commitment to the war effort. To ensure that the patriotism of the Russian people did not falter, Stalin's secret police and Communist Party commissars maintained rigid control over the Red Army. Supposed defeatism and cowardice were crushed ruthlessly. Between 1941 and 1942, for example, 157,593 men were executed for cowardice on the battlefield.

Stalin directed the war through the Supreme High Command (*Stavka Verkhnogo Glavnokomandovaniia*—Stavka) as commander-in-chief, supported by army officers and commissars. Stalin rarely left the Kremlin or ventured outside the USSR (he had a fear of flying). His only visits to the war zone, to the Western and Kalinin Fronts, were made on August 3 and 5, 1943, apparently for use in propaganda films. In common with Hitler, Stalin was loathe to sanction retreats (his refusal to pull back from Kiev in 1941 resulted in 660,000 Russians becoming prisoners of the Germans), but he did come to listen to commanders such as Zhukov about how battles and campaigns should be conducted. In late 1942, he had taken Zhukov's advice regarding how to trap the German Sixth Army at Stalingrad. The result had been a stunning Soviet victory that wiped out Axis forces in the Stalingrad Pocket. Similarly, in April 1943 Zhukov reported to Stalin concerning the situation in the Kursk salient, urging him to fight a defensive battle. Stalin took this advice, the Battle of Kursk was fought Zhukov's way, and the Germans were defeated.

On the road to victory

Kursk marked a turning point in the war on the Eastern Front, and so in 1943 the tragic theme of Soviet posters began to give way to more positive messages as towns and cities were liberated from the retreating Germans. There was also a growing thirst for revenge as enemy atrocities against the Soviet people were uncovered. By 1944, the chief poster theme was the forthcoming victory against the Nazis, with promises that the Red Army soldier would soon be in Berlin itself. They were not wrong. At the beginning of 1944, the Soviets deployed no fewer than 10 fronts, each one made up of between four and eight armies. The Red Army used no fewer than six tank armies during its subsequent operations in the Ukraine and Crimea. The Germans, outnumbered and outgunned, could only retreat in the face of this juggernaut. But the cost of victory was still heavy. To take Berlin itself, for example, cost the Red Army 77,000 killed and a further 272,000 wounded.

Though posters paid lip service to the alliance with the United States and Britain, Stalin viewed the Western Allies with suspicion, often accusing them of postponing the second front because they wanted to see the USSR bled white. Always putting his own interests first, he made exorbitant demands when it came to Lend Lease supplies, and planned the final Soviet offensives of the war with a Russian-dominated postwar Europe in mind.

One vast war factory

It was fortunate for Stalin, and indeed the Western Allies, that the Soviet Union could, to use Stalin's own words, be turned into a "single war camp" reasonably quickly. Soviet industry was moved en masse into the eastern hinterlands in 1941, and again in 1942 when the Germans advanced into the Caucasus, thus saving it from capture or destruction. The Soviet economy was centrally planned, which meant that before the war economists and bureaucrats had experience of building industrial plants on greenfield sites and organizing the large-scale movements of workers. This experience facilitated the evacuation of hundreds of factories and tens of thousands of workers east to the Urals, to the Volga region, to Kazakhstan, and to Siberia in 1941 and 1942. When they were up and running these factories produced thousands of tanks, aircraft, and artillery pieces. Soviet production posters had one simple message: more weapons for the front. And the workers did produce more, month after month, year after year. It was a feat of endurance that has never been equalled.

The scale of Soviet sacrifice in the war is staggering. It is estimated that 35 million Russians lost their lives during and immediately after The Great Patriotic War (when many perished during the winter of 1945–1946 due to shortages of shelter in the war-ravaged western USSR). No other member of the Allied alliance could have withstood such losses and remained in the war.

OPPOSITE PAGE: "Revenge on the Nazi plunderers." Revenge for crimes committed by the Germans on Russian soil was a common Soviet poster theme during World War II. Russians needed little prompting when it came to revenge, especially after 1943 when the Red Army began to liberate areas formerly under Nazi control and discovered evidence of atrocities.

КЛЯНЕМСЯ МСТИТЬ
ГИТЛЕРОВСКИМ ЗАХВАТЧИКАМ !

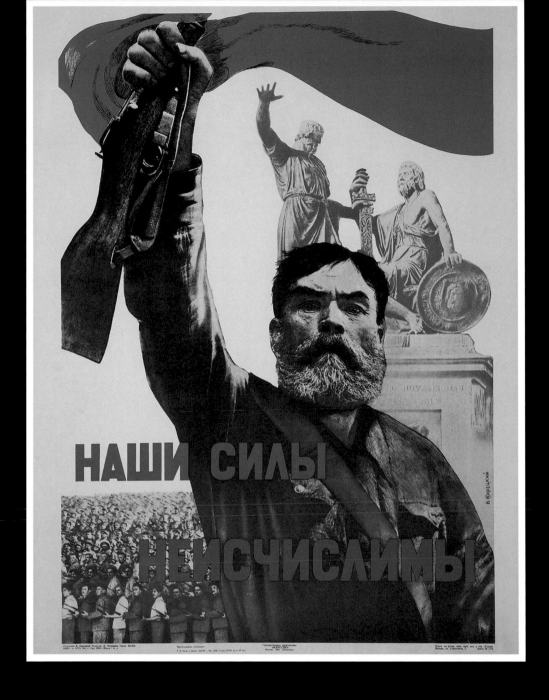

НАШИ СИЛЫ НЕИСЧИСЛИМЫ

В. КОРЕЦКИЙ

OPPOSITE PAGE: "We will mercilessly destroy and obliterate the enemy!" This 1941 poster shows a beast-like Hitler breaking through the German-Soviet Non-Aggression Pact of 1939. The pact had divided a conquered Poland between Germany and the Soviet Union, with the latter seizing the eastern half of the country. The pact and subsequent trade agreements between Berlin and Moscow seemed to suggest coexistence between two mutually exclusive ideologies. But on June 22, 1941, the Wehrmacht launched Operation Barbarossa, the invasion of the Soviet Union.

ABOVE: "Our forces are innumerable." This 1941 poster by Viktor Koretskii follows the theme of Soviet posters of early 1941: portraying the Soviet Union and its armed forces as stern, strong, and commanding. On paper the Red Army was very strong on the eve of Barbarossa: 5.5 million troops with over 29,000 tanks. In addition, the Red Air Force possessed 19,500 aircraft. However, in the 1941 campaign the Soviets lost 20,000 tanks and 10,000 combat aircraft. In addition, losses in troops were also huge. The Germans attacked on June 22. By July 9 the Red Army had lost nearly 750,000 killed, wounded, or missing.

BELOW: A Soviet satire on Hitler's ill-fated march on Moscow, showing the Blitzkrieg drum has finally burst. The text reads: "To Moscow! ho!; from Moscow: oh!" The poster is dated 1941, when German panzers were fast approaching Moscow. Indeed, they were only stopped at the beginning of December. The poster artist is Viktor Deni, who specialized in caricaturing the enemies of communism.

OPPOSITE PAGE: Initially, following the German attack, Soviet posters called on the people to defend the achievements of the 1917 Bolshevik Revolution. This 1941 poster by Vladimir Serov is an example of art with a socialist content. In 1932 Stalin had decreed that art should engage the proletariat and glorify the ideals and aims of the Party, with themes of progress and productivity, heroism, and hard work. The text reads: "Young men and women, defend the freedom, the nation, and the honor fought for you by your fathers."

ВСЕ СИЛЫ НА ЗАЩИТУ ГОРОДА ЛЕНИНА!

Opposite page: Iraklii Toidze's poster "The Motherland is calling You!" appeared shortly after the German invasion of the Soviet Union. A female figure representing Mother Russia holds the text of the Russian military oath in her right hand. In this poster a new trend in Soviet propaganda can be discerned. The conflict against Nazi Germany is not a war for communism but for the Motherland, the Slav nation. There is no mention of the word "Soviet" and no representation of hammer and sickles.

Above: A more traditional Soviet poster was this plea: "All forces to the defense of the city of Lenin!" Leningrad was an important Soviet armaments center (before the war it had been one of the most important centers for weapons production in the Soviet Union), as well as being home to 2.5 million people. The first German artillery shells fell on the city at the beginning of September 1941, heralding the start of a three-year siege. When the siege was lifted in 1944, between 1.6 and 2 million Russian soldiers and civilians had perished.

Below: "Our cause is just; victory will be ours." This 1941 poster printed in Leningrad depicts the great Russian hero Alexander Nevsky in white robes behind the ordinary Red Army soldier. Here the continuity between the war against Hitler and the earlier wars against the Teutonic Knights is stressed—the conflict between the Slavs and Germans that stretched back seven centuries. The poster is invoking a sense of history, Slav nationalism, and Russian patriotism.

Opposite page: "We will not abandon the achievements of October 1917!" This 1941 poster shows a Red Army soldier defeating his German foe, with a destroyed German tank in the bottom right-hand corner. Behind the battling soldier stand the achievements of the Soviet state: massive industrial plants and people's palaces of culture.

5

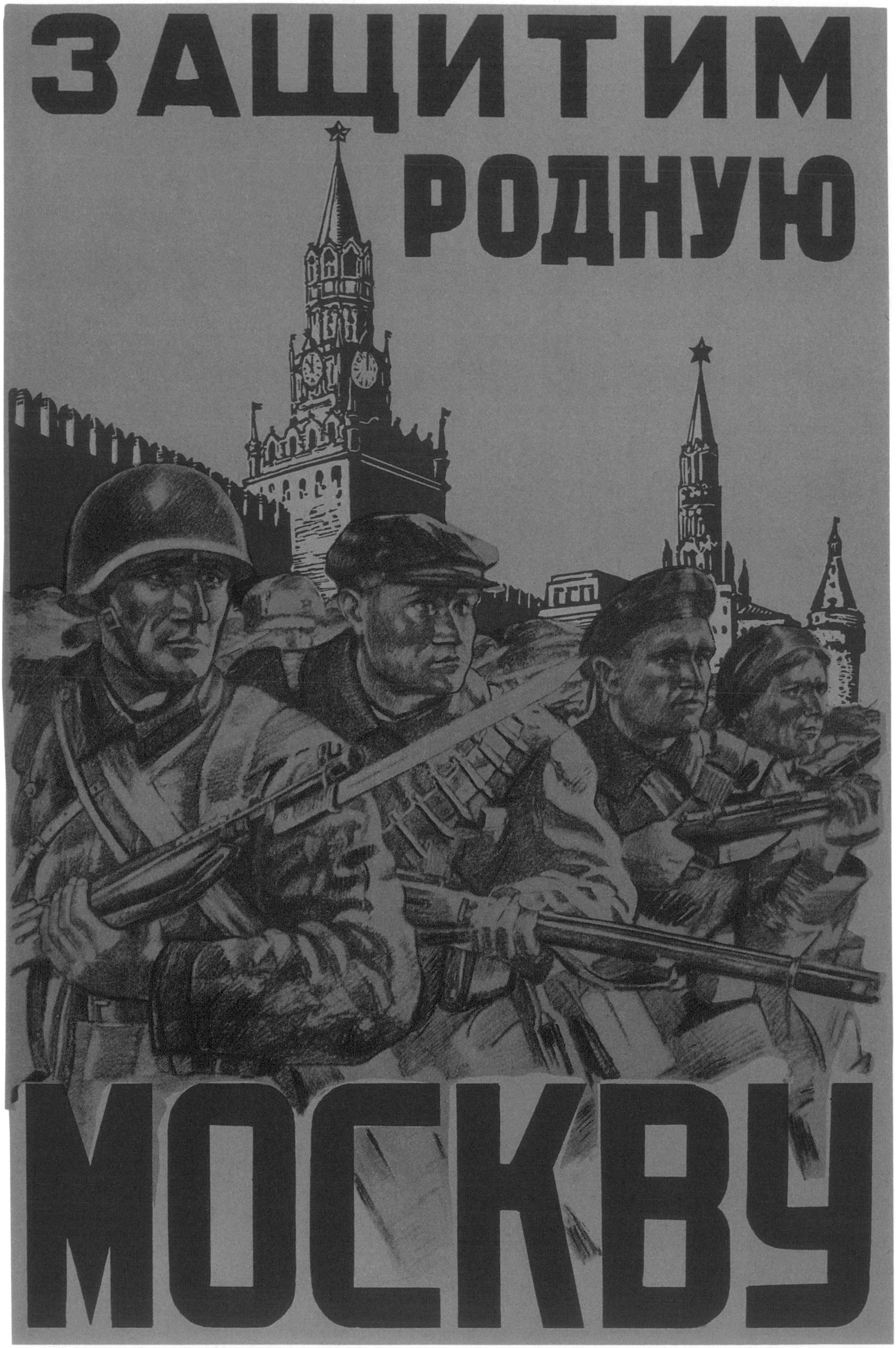
ЗАЩИТИМ
РОДНУЮ
МОСКВУ

БОЛЬШЕ МЕТАЛЛА —
БОЛЬШЕ ОРУЖИЯ !

1941

BELOW: A poster that places less emphasis on party propaganda and looks instead to the heroes of Russia history. "We will fight strongly, strike desperately—grandsons of Suvorov, children of Chapaev." Behind the Red Army tanks and soldiers are (from left to right): Alexander Nevsky, a thirteenth-century Russian prince who successfully fought the Swedes and Teutonic Knights; Alexander Suvorov (1729–1800), who fought the Poles, Turks, and French and never lost a battle; and Vasily Chapaev (1887–1919), a celebrated Bolshevik hero in the Russian Civil War who was killed fighting the Whites.

OPPOSITE PAGE: "We will take their places!" A 1941 poster by Vladimir Serov urging women to replace men in the factories. In 1941 the Soviet economy was faced with complete collapse as the Germans conquered the main industrial and agricultural regions of the USSR. The Soviet Union was reduced from being the world's third largest industrial economy, behind Germany and the United States, to the lower rank of industrial nations, such as Italy. But because of the exceptional efforts of Soviet workers, including millions of women, industry was rebuilt and war production increased. By 1943, women made up just over half the industrial workforce.

ЗАМЕНИМ!

Художник В. А. Серов.   Редактор Э. Л. Докторов.   И 76156   „Искусство“ № 1495 Индекс Р-10   Тираж 50000.   Заказ № 126   Государственное издательство „ИСКУССТВО“   Ленинград 1941 Москва   подписано к печати 5/VII 1941 г.   Объем 1 буж. л.   Цена 1 руб.   Полиграфическая лаборатория ЛОСХ. Ленинград, ул. Герцена 38   21

ВПЕРЕД! НА ЗАПАД!

Продублировано издательством «Плакат»   Первое издание осуществлено Государственным издательством «Искусство» в 1942 г.

САМООТВЕРЖЕННЫМ ТРУДОМ
ОБЕСПЕЧИМ КРАСНУЮ АРМИЮ
И ВОЕННО-МОРСКОЙ ФЛОТ
ВСЕМ НЕОБХОДИМЫМ
ДЛЯ ПОБЕДЫ НАД ВРАГОМ!

НАРОД и АРМИЯ НЕПОБЕДИМЫ!

Opposite page: "Forward! To the West!" This 1942 poster carries a common Soviet slogan during the war: the desire to liberate conquered Soviet territory and drive the fascists west. However, though the Red Army launched a number of offensives at the start of 1942 they all ended in failure. By the end of March 1942, the Red Army had suffered a total of 675,315 killed and missing and a staggering 1,179,457 wounded in these offensives.

Above: "The people and the army are unbeatable!" This poster stresses the close relationship between the soldier at the front and the factory worker who supplied him with weapons and ammunition. It was fortunate for Stalin that he was at the apex of a totalitarian regime. It was thus relatively simple for the country to be turned into a "single war camp" (Stalin's words). When war broke out all holidays and leave for workers was cancelled indefinitely, hours worked were fixed at between 12 and 16 each day, and three hours of compulsory

Урал фронту

ВОИН, ОТВЕТЬ РОДИНЕ ПОБЕДОЙ!

Первое издание осуществлено Государственным издательством «Искусство» в 1942 г.   Продублировано издательством «Плакат»

BELOW: "Every blow with the hammer is a blow against the enemy!" One thing that saved the Soviet Union in 1941 was the evacuation of hundreds of factories and tens of thousands of workers east to the Urals, to the Volga region, to Kazakhstan, and to Siberia. Between July and December 1941, 1,523 industrial enterprises, the majority steel, iron, and engineering plants, were transported east.

OPPOSITE PAGE: "Honor to the Soviet Air Force!" This 1943 poster celebrates the rebuilding of the Soviet Air Force after it was largely destroyed during Operation Barbarossa in 1941. The Russians built over 25,000 aircraft in 1942 and a further 34,900 in 1943. These efforts resulted in Soviet air superiority over the battlefield by mid-1943 on the Eastern Front.

СЛАВА СОВЕТСКОМУ ВОЗДУШНОМУ ФЛОТУ!

Автолитография П. Д. Магнушевского.   Редактор В. М. Свердлов.   Государственное издательство „ИСКУССТВО"   М—02288   № 2538   Тираж 3000 экз.   Цена 4 р.   Зак. № 1211 ЛТ УН-9
Ленинград 1943

Продублировано издательством «Плакат»

ЗА РОДИНУ-МАТЬ!

ВОИНЫ КРАСНОЙ АРМИИ!
КРЕПЧЕ УДАРЫ ПО ВРАГУ! ИЗГОНИМ НЕМЕЦКО-
ФАШИСТСКИХ МЕРЗАВЦЕВ С НАШЕЙ РОДНОЙ ЗЕМЛИ!

BELOW: "Over the enemy land to victory!" This 1943 image represents a change in the design and message of Soviet posters that reflected Red Army supremacy on the Eastern Front. The decisive victory at the Battle of Kursk in July 1943 gave the strategic initiative to the Red Army on the Eastern Front. The Germans never regained it. The Red Army had more soldiers, more tanks, and more artillery than the enemy, and in the second half of 1943 unleashed a series of hammer blows against the enemy that pushed the Germans west.

OPPOSITE PAGE: "Westwards!" A 1944 poster that reflects the Soviet victories in that year. A determined Red Army soldier knocks down an enemy sign saying "To the east" in German, signifying Soviet success in liberating conquered Russian territory. Gone are the calls to defend the Motherland or "our beloved Moscow." For the Germans, 1944 was one long catastrophe on the Eastern Front, and by the end of the year the Red Army was nearing the border of Germany itself.

ВОИНУ-ПОБЕДИТЕЛЮ —
ВСЕНАРОДНАЯ ЛЮБОВЬ!

Продублировано издательством «Плакат»   Первое издание осуществлено Государственным издательством «Искусство» в 1944 г.

КРЕПЧЕ УДАРЫ ПО ВРАГУ!

**ОСВОБОДИМ РОДНЫЕ ГОРОДА И СЕЛА
ОТ ФАШИСТСКОЙ НЕЧИСТИ!**

Opposite page: A 1944 poster with the message: "A nation's love to the victorious soldier!" By 1944 it was clear to the Soviet authorities that the German Army would be defeated on the Eastern Front, and that its armies would be able to launch an assault on Nazi Germany itself. The grim-faced and battered soldiers that adorned the posters of 1941 and 1942 were gone. Now the faces of Red Army soldiers were either determined or happy, because they knew that they would be victorious in the near future.

Above: "Stronger blows against the enemy! We will free our country's cities and villages from the fascist vermin!" This 1944 poster produced in Leningrad displays the hatred for the German invaders, and how Soviet propaganda dehumanized the German enemy. The conflict was repeatedly described as a war of annihilation in which all Germans must be exterminated, in much the same way as one destroys rats and other vermin. In this the Germans were reaping the whirlwind they had sown, for they had waged a war of extermination against the "subhuman" Bolshevik Slav enemy.

Below: A 1944 poster that declares "We will get to Berlin!" The Red Army's Operation Bagration in June, which shattered the German Army Group Center, involved 2.5 million troops, 5,200 tanks, and 5,300 aircraft. Army Group Center numbered only 580,000 troops and 900 tanks. The offensive was a great Soviet victory, which caused the Germans to fall back west into Poland.

Opposite page: "So it will be with the fascist beast!" This poster is dated 1945, by which date the Red Army was about to launch its campaign to bring the war on the Eastern Front to an end. The poster shows the flags of the three main members of the Grand Alliance: the Soviet Union, the United States, and Britain. Of the three, it was the Soviet Union that had the largest armed forces fighting the Germans, with 11,500,000 troops deployed on the Eastern Front at the beginning of 1945.

ДОЙДЕМ ДО БЕРЛИНА!

ТАК БУДЕТ
С ФАШИСТСКИМ ЗВЕРЕМ!

1941–1945

ПОДВИГ
НАРОДА
БЕССМЕРТЕН

Opposite page: "Honor to the victorious soldier!" With the war against Nazi Germany won, Soviet posters reverted to type, with the hammer and sickle returned to prominence and little reference to nationalism and patriotism. Nevertheless, the poster rightly salutes the efforts of the ordinary Red Army soldier, whose selfless sacrifice had enabled the Soviet Union to win the war against Nazi Germany.

Above: A post-war poster created by Nina Vatolina, an artist who produced many posters both during the war and afterward. The title, "The victory of the people is eternal, 1941–1945," is a celebration of the population's efforts in World War II. It was worth celebrating. The scale of the destruction and loss of life inflicted on the USSR during four years of brutal warfare is difficult to comprehend. Estimates vary, but it is reckoned that 35 million Russians lost their lives during the Russo-German War.

chapter 7

United States Posters

Of all the warring nations in World War II, it was the United States that benefitted the most from the conflict. In 1941, even before she had entered the war, the United States produced more steel, aluminium, oil, and motor vehicles than all the other major nations put together. A sleeping giant before the war, by the end of it the United States was the world's greatest power, both militarily and economically. In 1941 the country was essentially a civilian economy; by 1945 it was a manufacturing collossus, having produced 297,000 aircraft, 193,000 artillery pieces, 86,000 tanks, 2 million trucks, 8,800 naval vessels, and 87,000 landing craft.

The OWI

Such a massive war effort demanded an equally large mobilization of the working population. And so the Office of War Information (OWI) was created in 1942 to be the U.S. Government propaganda agency during the war, responsible for turning the country into the "arsenal of democracy." The OWI established systems of distribution modeled upon the volunteer organizations that had been established in World War I. Posters were distributed by post offices, railroad stations, schools, restaurants, and retail store groups. The OWI also organized distribution through volunteer defense councils, whose members took the "Poster Pledge." The "Poster Pledge" urged volunteers to "avoid waste," treat posters "as real war ammunition," "never let a poster lie idle," and "make every one count to the fullest extent."

During the war the OWI developed a number of major propaganda themes for use in posters and the media in general. Immediately after the attack on Pearl Harbor (December 7, 1941) American propaganda focused on the nature of the enemy. In many publications the Japanese became the "yellow peril," and in an article on the Pearl Harbor attack, *Time* magazine talked of "the yellow bastards." In fact, the Japanese had always been viewed with suspicion. Immigration into the United States from Asia began in earnest during the early-mid 1800s, mainly in the form of Chinese laborers seeking employment in manual industries. Japanese immigration gained pace in the late 1800s, with many Japanese immigrants heading for employment on plantations in Hawaii. By 1929, there were 230,000 Japanese immigrants in the United States, most of them concentrated along the West Coast of California. There they joined thousands of Chinese workers, and around 24,000 Filipinos also arrived in California in the 1920s.

The "yellow peril"

From the moment they arrived, Asian-Americans were perceived to be a threat to American society and values, and they were branded the "yellow peril."

War posters likened the Japanese to animals such as apes, snakes, and rats, thus dehumanizing the enemy. This image was helped by the actions of the Japanese themselves. In April 1942, for example, 78,000 U.S. and Filipino troops surrendered to the Japanese in the Philippines. During the march from Bataan to Camp O'Donnell, north of Manila, the guards deprived the prisoners of food and water, and murdered any stragglers. According to the Bushido code, soldiers who surrendered rather than fight to the death dishonored themselves and forfeited any right to humane treatment. To make matters worse, the captives had previously subsisted for months on partial rations, which meant many started out in a weakened state. Alf Larson was one of those Americans who endured the march and who later recorded his experiences during the "Bataan Death March."

Japanese atrocities

"If people would fall down and couldn't go any further, the Japanese would either bayonet or shoot them. They also would bayonet prisoners who couldn't keep up. Those who stepped out of line or had fallen out of the ranks were beaten with clubs and/or rifle butts. Some American prisoners who couldn't keep up were run over by Japanese vehicles. I saw the remains of an American soldier who had been run over by a tank. I didn't see the actual event but the Japanese just left his remains in the middle of the road. We could see them as we walked by. Wounded Americans were expected to keep up like everyone else, regardless of their condition. But, some wounded prisoners just couldn't go on. They were either bayoneted, beat with clubs, rifle butts, or shot. Some soldiers had diarrhea so bad that they couldn't keep up and the Japanese shot them. As we walked along, we could see the bodies of decomposing American soldiers and Filipino women who had been mutilated and obviously raped. I'm sure the dogs in the area got fat!" Such atrocities encouraged hatred among the U.S. public.

Posters also sounded a call to arms for the American people. They proclaimed that the United States had been viciously attacked and would not sit by and do nothing. "Avenge December 7" was a powerful message. But the United States was not simply fighting

ABOVE: J. Howard Miller's famous poster of Rosie the Riveter, "We Can Do It!" The image was modeled on Michigan factory worker Geraldine Doyle in 1942. Rosie the Riveter became an American cultural icon and came to represent the more than six million women in U.S. war factories during World War II. They made a crucial contribution to the eventual Allied victory.

Japan because of Pearl Harbor. It was also fighting against Japanese imperialist expansionism in Asia. This was a clever argument, because although the United States was not a colonizing nation, it still had authority over the entire Philippines (a legacy of its victory in the Spanish-American War of 1898) and had powerful commercial and religious interests throughout China. European and U.S. territory combined meant that the West dominated much of Pacific Asia's natural resources. Nevertheless, the idea that the United States was fighting for peace and democracy was a powerful motivator for the American people.

The just war

The liberation of oppressed peoples was also a theme of U.S. posters: to free Europe of Nazism and Asia of Japanese imperialism. For a religious people, the conviction that they were fighting a "just war" simplified things for Americans. Indeed, President Roosevelt himself was deeply religious.

Before Pearl Harbor, not all Americans were enthusiastic about joining the war. Indeed, there was spontaneous and widespread opposition to Franklin Roosevelt's obvious attempts to embroil the United States in the European war that broke out in 1939. That opposition was centered in the America First Committee. The organization had 800,000 members at its height, and had four main beliefs. First, that the United States should build an impregnable defense for America. Second, no foreign powers, nor group of powers, could successfully attack a prepared America. Third, American democracy could be preserved only by keeping out of the European war. Fourth, "Aid short of war" weakened national defense at home and threatened to involve America in war abroad. Following the attack on Pearl Harbor, on December 11, 1941, the national committee of the America First Committee voted to disband the organization.

To fight a just war against both Germany and Japan required large armed forces and massive quantities of tanks, ships, aircraft, and armaments. This meant factory production on a mass scale. The United States was a democracy whose population was accustomed to a high standard of living. Unlike in Soviet Russia, the people could not be forced to work in factories or agriculture. Posters encouraging individuals to produce more, buy war bonds, and become volunteers therefore stressed the linkage between the factory worker and the frontline soldier. The posters also stressed the patriotic nature of these efforts. "Production, America's answer," "More production," and "let's give him enough and on time" all stressed the dependence of the armed forces on factory workers. One of the most famous production posters, "Give it your best!," was simply the American flag with the words underneath.

The campaign worked. The U.S. became an industrial giant that poured out guns, tanks, aircraft, and ships at a phenomenal rate, and in the end this was always going to be decisive. Prefabricated merchant vessels, known as Liberty Ships, were constructed at the rate of one per day at the height of the war. At the Battle of the Philippine Sea in 1944, American Admiral Marc Mitscher was happy to let his attack aircraft ditch in the sea, provided he could recover the pilots, because there were more than sufficient planes in reserve. At this battle Japanese naval aviation suffered a blow from which it never recovered. After this, the extreme courage of Japanese sailors and airmen, and their willingness to sacrifice themselves in their cause, proved fruitless. The *kamikaze* pilots inflicted great losses on the U.S. Navy (especially during the battle for Okinawa), but the issue was by then not in doubt. The greatest naval struggle in history had been won by the United States.

Aid to allies

As well as equipping its own armed forces, the United States was able to send valuable aid to the Soviet Union. Lend Lease assistance became crucial to the Red Army in the last two years of the war. Between 1943 and 1945, Western aid, specifically trucks, rail engines, and rail wagons, allowed the Red Army to maintain the momentum of its offensives by transporting troops and supplies to reinforce breakthrough armies, thus denying the Germans time to organize fresh defense lines and escape encirclements. These were the quantities of goods supplied to the Russians: armored vehicles: 12,161; guns and mortars: 9,600; combat aircraft: 18,303; aircraft engines: 14,902; trucks and jeeps: 312,600; explosives: 325,784 tons (330,997 tonnes); locomotives: 1,860; rail cars: 11,181; field telephones: 422,000; foodstuffs: 4,281,910 tons (4,350,420 tonnes); oil: 2,599,000 tons (2,640,584 tonnes); and boots: 15,000,000 pairs.

The development of the atomic bomb symbolized America's vast economic might. The "Manhattan Project" was the codename for the U.S. atomic weapons program. The origins of the project went back to 1939, when top U.S. scientists, including the influential Albert Einstein, persuaded President Roosevelt of the military possibilities for fission chain reactions of atomic elements. Official work began in February 1940 with a grant of $6,000, but on December 6, 1941—with war raging in Europe and threatening in the Far East—the program was upgraded and placed under the jurisdiction of the Office of Scientific Research and Development. The War Department took joint management following the Japanese attack on Pearl Harbor. The program assumed the name Manhattan Project in 1942, after the U.S. Army engineers of the Manhattan district who were given the task of constructing the initial plants for the work. On July 16, 1945, the first atomic bomb was exploded at Alamogordo, New Mexico. The U.S., having invested two billion dollars in the Manhattan Project, now had its atomic bomb. The British had dropped out of atomic bomb research in 1942 in recognition that they lacked the industrial resources to pursue such a project.

The birth of a superpower

The aircraft that dropped the atomic bomb, the B-29 Superfortress, was also indicative of America's vast technological and economic resources. The B-29 was designed as an extreme long-range "Hemisphere Defense Weapon." When it entered service in July 1943, this huge 10-crew bomber had a range of 4,100 miles (6,598 km) and a bomb load of 20,000 lb (9,072 kg). It was an advanced aircraft—the gun turrets dotted around the fuselage were controlled remotely by gunners sitting inside the fuselage who aimed the weapons via periscopes. The B-29 was ideal for the vast distances of the Pacific theater. Some 3,970 B-29s were produced during the war.

The campaign to mobilize the American people to fight the war had been a great victory. The civilian workforce grew from 46.5 million in 1940 to 55 million by 1945, notwithstanding that the American armed forces by this date numbered 11 million. American farms had, in the same period, increased their production by 22 percent with a diminishing number of farmers. By such efforts had the American people helped to destroy the Axis war effort.

OPPOSITE PAGE: The America First Committee (AFC) was established in September 1940. Its aim was to keep the United States out of the European war and it was opposed to sending aid to the British, its supporters arguing that to do so would weaken home defense and might suck America into the conflict. At its height the AFC had 800,000 members. However, it was dissolved a few days after the Japanese attack on Pearl Harbor.

WAR'S FIRST CASUALTY

AMERICA FIRST COMMITTEE

141 West Jackson Boulevard
CHICAGO

I WANT YOU *for the* **U.S. ARMY ENLIST NOW**

OPPOSITE PAGE: The entry of the United States into the war required a massive increase in the size of the armed forces. In this Tom Woodburn poster Uncle Sam, standing in front of an unfurled American flag, rolls up his sleeves ready for a fight. The image symbolizes America's reluctance to get involved in the war, but her determination to win once hostilities had commenced. The army

ABOVE: This poster by the artist and writer James Montgomery Flagg is one of the most iconic recruiting posters of the twentieth century. During World War I Flagg designed 46 posters for the government. This included the famous Uncle Sam poster with the caption "I Want You for the U.S. Army." An adapted version of this poster was also used during World War II. In this poster Flagg used a version of his own face

BELOW: The Office of Civilian Defense (OCD) was headed by New York Mayor Fiorello LaGuardia. He chose the popular First Lady Eleanor Roosevelt as his assistant. By November 1940, all the states and 5,935 towns and cities had set up defense councils. This is a poster sponsored by the Philadelphia Council of Defense calling for volunteers to become air raid wardens, auxiliary firemen, auxiliary policemen, and other "services in the civilian army."

OPPOSITE PAGE: Before the United States entered the war, President Roosevelt described America as being in a "a state of unlimited emergency." As a result, he advised each city to organize its own "civil defense" system to plan and prepare for the dangers looming on the horizon. On May 20, 1941, Roosevelt created the Office of Civilian Defense (OCD) to oversee and assist this task. When war broke out, thousands of civil defense chapters were organized by volunteers across the country.

AMERICA CALLING

Take your place in
CIVILIAN DEFENSE
CONSULT YOUR NEAREST DEFENSE COUNCIL

DIVISION OF INFORMATION, OFFICE FOR EMERGENCY MANAGEMENT

☆ U. S. GOVERNMENT PRINTING OFFICE : 1941—O—423471

VOLUNTEER
CIVILIAN DEFENSE

Opposite page: This poster encourages the owners of small boats to enlist in the U.S. Coast Guard. The Coast Guard was ordered to operate as part of the U.S. Navy in November 1941, and thereafter its personnel crewed amphibious ships and landing craft, landing soldiers and U.S. Marines on beaches in North Africa, Italy, France, and the

Above: A poster issued in Alabama encouraging voluntary participation in civilian defense. The image is of an aircraft flying over the outline of the state. Throughout the state civilian defense councils ran courses instructing volunteers in how to enforce blackouts and the procedures for air raid warnings. The first state-wide blackout was held

Man the
GUNS
Join the NAVY

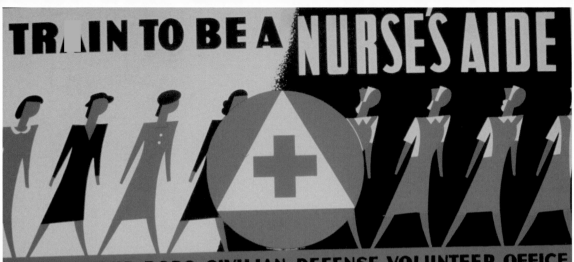

BELOW: The U.S. Marine Corps was an elite force, and before the war it was highly selective concerning new recruits. In 1939, for example, out of 36,356 applicants, only 5,861 became Marines. An official U.S. Navy publication noted: "Marine recruiting officers opened their doors on 8 December 1941 to find long lines of young men eager to join the Marines. In the days that followed, there was no slacking off in the numbers seeking to enlist."

OPPOSITE PAGE: A U.S. Marine recruiting poster of 1942 that is much more aggressive in tone than the one below. This reflects the sense of outrage felt in America concerning Japan's nefarious attack on Pearl Harbor and subsequent Japanese victories in the Pacific in early 1942. In this poster, Marines with bayonets fixed to their rifles are hunting the enemy in the jungle. Young Americans joined the U.S. Marines in droves in the war. For example, a total of 44,947 new recruits had joined during the period December 1, 1941, to February, 28, 1942.

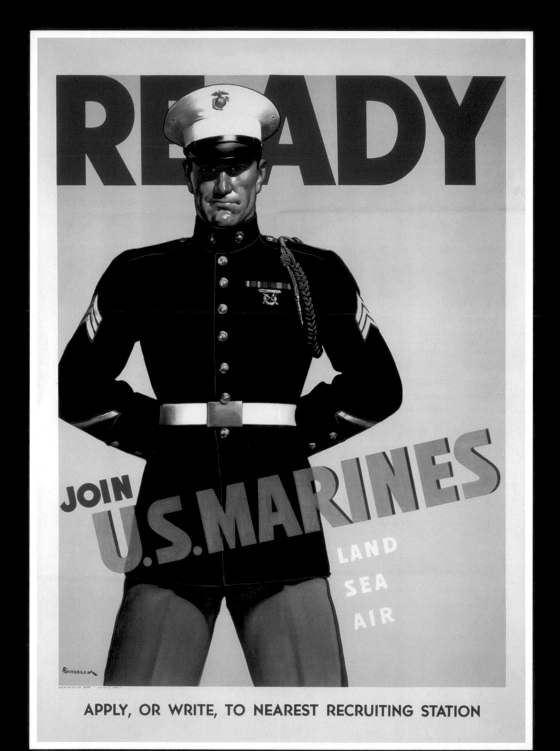

LET'S GO GET 'EM !

U.S. MARINES

Beck Engraving Co., Phila., Pa., Reqn.—469-1943, 7-11-42, 50M.

BELOW: A recruiting poster by David Stone Martin of the African American war hero Doris "Dorie" Miller, who won the Navy Cross for his actions at Pearl Harbor on board the USS *West Virginia*. His citation reads: "Miller, despite enemy strafing and bombing and in the face of a serious fire, assisted in moving his Captain, who had been mortally wounded, to a place of greater safety, and later manned and operated a machine gun directed at enemy Japanese attacking aircraft until ordered to leave the bridge." Doris "Dorie" Miller was killed in the Pacific in 1943.

OPPOSITE PAGE: A 1943 poster encouraging women to undertake war work. The image is of a woman working in an aircraft factory and is based on an Alfred T. Palmer photograph. Palmer was a photographer and film maker who was the official photographer for the United States Merchant Marine and later for major shipping lines. During the war he was appointed head photographer for the Office of War Information by President Roosevelt.

I'm Proud... my husband
wants me to do my part

SEE YOUR U. S. EMPLOYMENT SERVICE
WAR MANPOWER COMMISSION

OPPOSITE PAGE: The Women's Army Corps (WAC) was created for the "purpose of making available to the national defense the knowledge, skill, and special training of the women of the nation." Applicants had to be U.S. citizens between the ages of 21 and 45 with no dependents, be at least five feet tall, and weigh 100 pounds or more. The recruits served in the United States and overseas, as stenographers, typists, translators, legal secretaries, cryptographers, telegraph and teletype operators, and radiographers. In total, over 150,000 American women

ABOVE: The idea that women working outside the home was a patriotic act is illustrated in this poster. A women in working clothes, supported by her husband, stands in front of the American flag. At first, neither husbands nor the government wanted married women to work. Husbands viewed a woman's role as being in the home. In addition, women with children under 14 were encouraged to stay home to care for their families because the government feared that a rise in working mothers would lead to a rise in juvenile delinquency.

1935 Neutrality Act to arm U.S. ships for defense against Axis attacks
The Committee dissolved itself in January 1942 after the entry of the
United States in the war.

HELP BRITAIN
DEFEND AMERICA

SPEED PRODUCTION

COMMITTEE TO DEFEND AMERICA BY AIDING THE ALLIES

This poster illustrates one of the common techniques used by American propaganda during the war: to liken the Japanese to animals such as rats and snakes.

Above: This simple 1941 poster by Jean Carlu emphasizes America's industrial might. Carlu originally began training as an architect, but turned to commercial art after an accident in which he lost his right arm. During the 1920s and 1930s he was a leading figure in French poster design. In 1940, he was in the United States organizing an exhibition at the New York World's Fair for the French Information Service when Paris fell to the Germans. This poster was voted poster of the year in 1941.

Opposite page: This poster illustrates one of the common techniques used by American propaganda during the war: to liken the Japanese to animals such as rats and snakes. There were a number of drives for scrap during the war. In July 1941, for example, the Office of Production Management announced a two-week drive to collect aluminum cookware and other items to make aircraft. The response was massive. Unfortunately, it was discovered that only virgin aluminum was suitable to make aircraft. And so the pots and pans collected were made into—pots and pans.

BELOW: This poster reflects the diverse composition of the United States in the 1940s, and that everyone should come together in a unified effort to defeat the enemy. Not everyone was welcome, however. For example, there were around eight million German-Americans in the United States, and during the war the government used many methods to control them. They included internment, individual and group exclusion from military zones, internee exchanges, deportation, repatriation, "alien enemy" registration, travel restrictions, and property confiscation.

OPPOSITE PAGE: In this Maurice Merlin poster, employment opportunities for farm and industrial laborers are announced. However, the appeal for manpower could not fulfil Michigan's requirements. Therefore, in 1944 and 1945 between 4,000 and 5,000 prisoners of war worked on the state's farms. Prisoners, Italians and Germans, usually worked six-day, 48-hour weeks. They lived in tented camps surrounded by simple wooden fences.

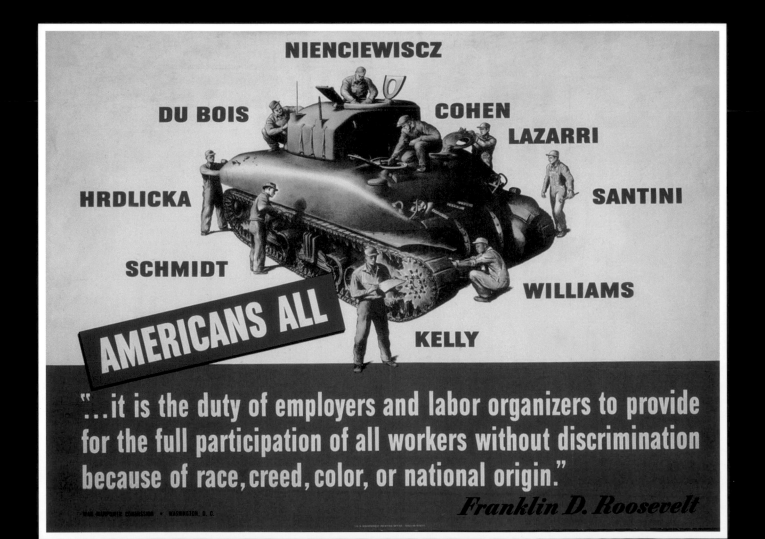

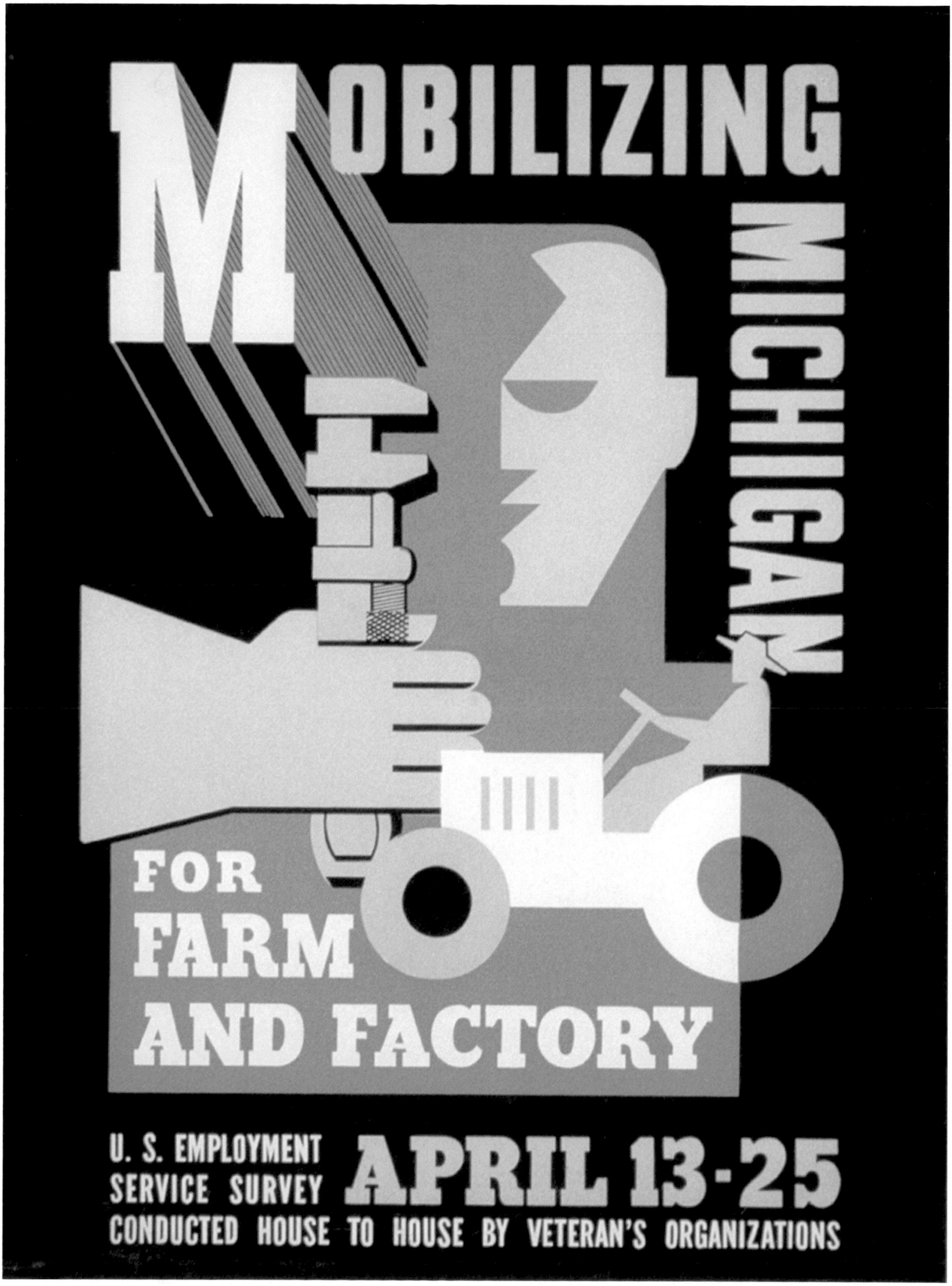
MOBILIZING
MICHIGAN
FOR
FARM
AND FACTORY
U. S. EMPLOYMENT
SERVICE SURVEY
APRIL 13-25
CONDUCTED HOUSE TO HOUSE BY VETERAN'S ORGANIZATIONS

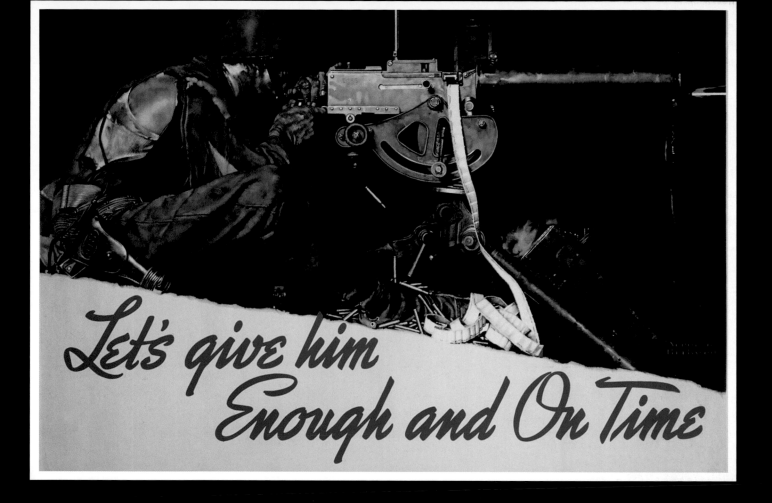

Let's give him Enough and On Time

OPPOSITE PAGE: This simple poster shows a bomb heading toward the sun of the Japanese flag, which also has a swastika at its center. The artist Zudor thus shows that Japan and Germany are the common enemies and that American production will destroy them both. It was commissioned by the War Production Board. In May 1942 Vice President Henry G. Wallace stated: "Hitler knows as well as those of us who sit in on the War Production Board meetings that we here in the United States are winning the battle of production. He knows that both labor and business in the United States are doing a most remarkable job and that his only hope is to crash through to a complete victory some time during the next six months."

ABOVE: This 1942 poster by Norman Rockwell stresses the dependence of the frontline soldier on the factory worker. Of the design Rockwell said: "When, during the recent war, the Ordnance Department gave me the suggestion for this poster, I made a rough sketch which was approved by the Army. Then a neighbor of mine, Colonel Fairfax Ayers, a retired Army officer, arranged to have a gun crew and machine gun sent to my studio. They arrived in a jeep, to the great excitement of our Arlington boys. The gunner insisted that I picture his gun in gleaming good order, but he let me rip his shirt. This final poster represents one of our grand soldiers in a tough spot on the firing line. The coil of cartridge tape and the empty cartridges show that he is about down

BELOW: This Charles Coiner poster of 1942, intended to boost war production, is a very effective design that combines a motto with the American flag. Before the war Coiner designed the Blue Eagle symbol for the National Recovery Administration. This was a federal agency created to encourage industrial recovery and combat unemployment under the Roosevelt administration. During World War II, he designed posters such as this one for the Office of War Information.

OPPOSITE PAGE: This poster was created by the photographer Roy Schatt, who started as an illustrator for government agencies in the 1930s, under the presidency of Franklin D. Roosevelt. In addition to his poster work, Schatt directed shows during World War II while with the U.S. Army's special forces in India. However, he is best known for his portraits of movie icon James Dean taken in the 1950s.

GIVE IT YOUR BEST!

OFFICE OF WAR INFORMATION
POSTER NO. 9   WASHINGTON D.C.

LIBERTY FOR ALL

KEEP 'EM FLYING

PENNA ART W.P.A.

OPPOSITE PAGE: This appeal for binoculars (including ones made by the German firm Zeiss) reflects the shortage of binoculars in the U.S. Navy in early 1942. The United States had only one premier binocular manufacturer, Bausch & Lomb of Rochester, New York. The government decided to nationalize the company to safeguard the supply of binocular manufacturers. Interestingly, Bausch & Lomb was founded in 1853 by Germans John Jacob Bausch and Henry Lomb.

ABOVE: The Statue of Liberty had been used in American posters in World War I. It was used again in World War II, symbolizing as it did a patriotic America strong in the face of foreign aggression. To promote support for the war, artists incorporated the Statue of Liberty in their poster designs. This is a 1943 poster by Albina Garlinski, in which Liberty shares the stage with an aircraft carrier and warplanes.

BELOW. One of the many posters calling for scrap drives that appeared during the war. In 1942, there were two scrap drives in San Francisco alone, in September and October. Though the scrap drives were hugely successful, some went overboard. For example, in addition to old streetcar tracks, wrought iron fences, and church bells, people also donated relics of previous conflicts, such as cannons, park statues, and other war memorials.

OPPOSITE PAGE. This poster is encouraging skilled laborers to join the Seabees, the Naval Construction Force that built advanced bases in w zones. On December 28, 1941, Rear Admiral Ben Moreell requested specific authority to raise naval construction units, and on January 5, 1942, he gained authority from the Bureau of Navigation to recruit men from the construction trades for assignment to a Naval Construction Regiment composed of three Naval Construction Battalions. This was the beginning of the famous Seabees.

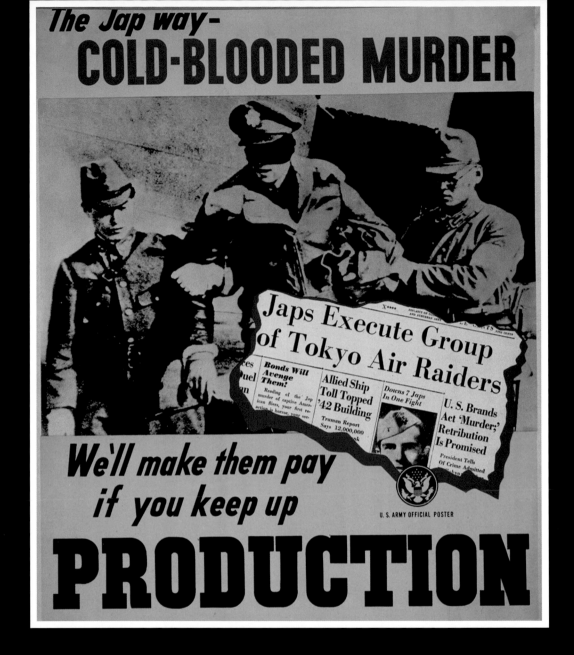

The Jap way—
COLD-BLOODED MURDER

Japs Execute Group of Tokyo Air Raiders

We'll make them pay if you keep up **PRODUCTION**

U.S. ARMY OFFICIAL POSTER

Opposite page: The Office of War Information sponsored this 1943 poster, which shows factory workers at an integrated aircraft plant during World War II. Executive Order 8802, issued in June 1941, prohibited government contractors from engaging in employment discrimination based on race, color, or national origin. This resulted in tens of thousands of African Americans, both men and women, being able to find work in war production.

Above: This poster makes use of the Japanese execution of three U.S. Air Force personnel who were captured after the Doolittle raid against Japan in April 1942. The raid had boosted morale in both America and Britain, and the trial and subsequent execution of three men by the Japanese outraged Allied public opinion. This poster makes use of this sense of outrage to promise retribution against Japan "if you keep up production."

UNITED
we are strong

UNITED we will win

NEIGHBORHOOD FINGERPRINT STATION

FINGERPRINTS ARE YOUR IDENTIFICATION AND PROTECTION DURING WARTIME HAVE THE ENTIRE FAMILY TAKE THEIRS NOW!

WAR IDENTIFICATION BUREAU-CDVO

BLACKOUT *means* BLACK

ISSUED BY THE OAKLAND DEFENSE COUNCIL
WPA ART PROGRAM

OPPOSITE PAGE: This poster stresses the importance of having finger-prints on file as a form of identification. Some groups had no choice in the matter. "Enemy aliens," for example, were required to register and be fingerprinted. They could also be imprisoned. The Enemy Alien Act of 1798 authorized the jailing of any citizen of a country with which the United States was at war, based solely on their nationality, and irrespective of their loyalty or conduct. In World War II, this was extended to U.S. citizens of Japanese descent, 70,000 of whom were interned during the war.

ABOVE: This poster issued by California's Oakland Defense Council reminds citizens of the need for complete blackouts as part of civil defense procedures. People needed little convincing. Immediately after Pearl Harbor the residents of the state feared a Japanese invasion. The state's beaches were strung with miles of barbed wire, coastal cites were blacked out, and citizens sandbagged their homes and businesses. Radio stations went off the air, commercial airliners were grounded, and ships were ordered to stay in port. The invasion never came, but Californians remained jittery well into 1942.

Below: The artist Edward T. Grigware was a War Record painter for the U. S. Navy during World War II. He did much of his work on the aircraft carrier USS *Enterprise* during the Pacific campaigns. He also produced a number of posters. This poster was issued by the Thirteenth Naval District, which consisted of the geographic areas of Washington, Oregon, Idaho, Montana, and Wyoming.

Opposite page: A variation on the "careless talk costs lives" and "loose lips sink ships" themes. In this Frederick Siebel poster a drowning sailor points accusingly. It was one of many American posters which warned against careless chatter concerning the locations of troops or ships. These posters were displayed in shipyards, army and navy posts, waterfront bars, and restaurants.

LET ME DO THE TALKING!

HOMER
ANSLEY

SERVE IN SILENCE

ISSUED BY THE SAN FRANCISCO JUNIOR CHAMBER OF COMMERCE

OPPOSITE PAGE: This poster reminds citizens to be mindful of careless talk and to let the military speak for the nation. It was designed by Homer Ansley, who worked for a billboard company before the war. The large howitzer in the poster symbolizes America's large output of weaponry to fight the Axis alliance.

ABOVE: This poster suggests that careless communication may be harmful to the war effort, showing a train blowing up, presumably as a result of sabotage by enemy agents. This poster was issued in Missouri, which during the war received more than 15,000 German and Italian prisoners of war. The initial reaction to enemy prisoners was often hostile, with many fearing the enemy in their midst. However, Missouri farmers experienced an extreme shortage of manpower for planting, tending, and harvesting their crops, and the prisoners proved extremely useful in alleviating this situation.

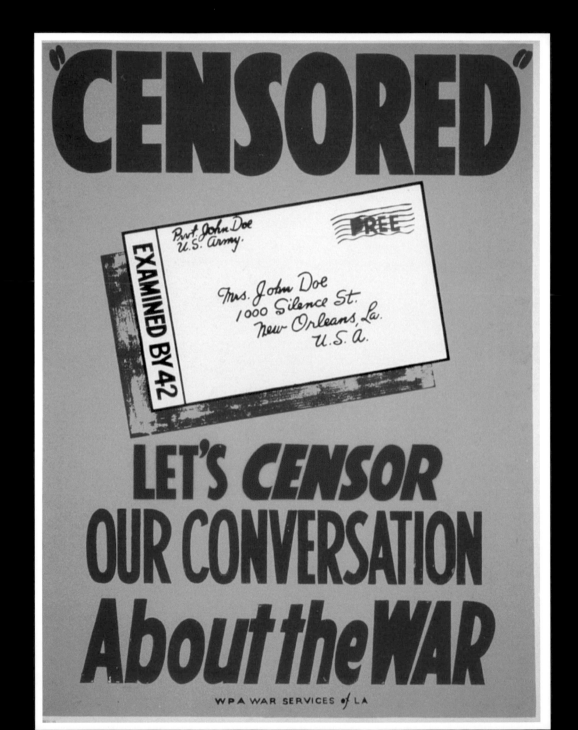

ANTON OTTO FISCHER

a careless word...

A NEEDLESS LOSS

I PLEDGE ALLEGIANCE

and

SILENCE

ABOUT THE WAR

WPA WAR SERVICES of LA.

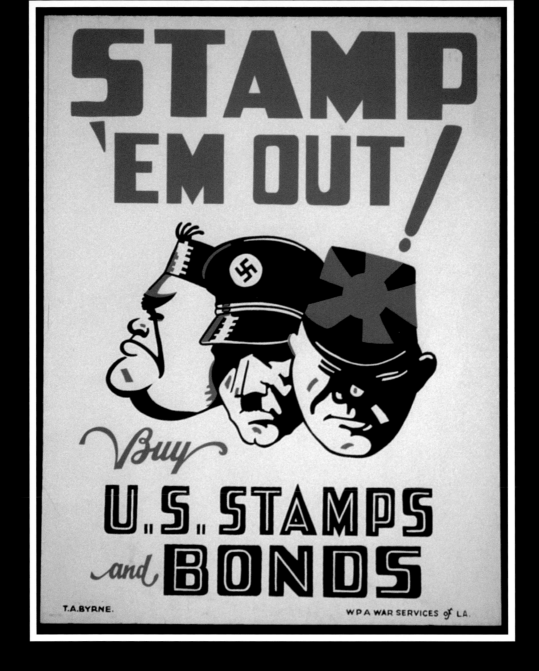

STAMP 'EM OUT!

Buy

U.S. STAMPS and BONDS

T.A.BYRNE.

WPA WAR SERVICES of LA.

BELOW: A 1942 poster with a simple message. The campaign to convince Americans to purchase war bonds was incredibly successful. By the end of World War II, over 85 million Americans had invested in war bonds—a total of $185.7 billion of securities. As well as financing the war effort, war bonds were designed to reduce consumer spending in order to lessen inflationary pressures and black market activity. Selling war bonds was also designed to raise morale by creating a sense of participation in the war effort.

OPPOSITE PAGE: As with posters that stressed the link between the factory worker and the frontline soldier, this war bonds poster is stressing the same interdependence. There was great pressure on civilians to purchase war bonds and to be seen supporting the "boys" fighting the enemy. No one wanted to be branded a "mattress stuffer" who hoarded money instead of purchasing bonds.

He Gives 100%
You Can Lend 10%

JOHN M° CRADY

SAVE FREEDOM OF WORSHIP

EACH ACCORDING TO THE DICTATES
OF HIS OWN CONSCIENCE

NORMAN ROCKWELL

BUY WAR BONDS

OPPOSITE PAGE: A war bonds poster that uses the image of a Tuskegee Airman. The Tuskegee Airmen were named after an African American squadron based in Tuskegee, Alabama, in 1941. African American pilots proved their worth during the war, winning 150 Distinguished Flying Crosses, 744 Air Medals, 8 Purple Hearts, and 14 Bronze Stars. It is a sobering thought that, despite the efforts of African Americans in World War II, the U.S. armed forces were not desegregated until 1948.

ABOVE: A poster of a Norman Rockwell painting, one of his "Four Freedoms" series of paintings he created during the war. In January 1941 President Roosevelt made a speech to Congress, stating: "We look forward to a world founded upon four essential human freedoms. The first is freedom of speech and expression—everywhere in the world. The second is freedom of every person to worship God in his own way—everywhere in the world. The third is freedom from want—everywhere in the world. The fourth is freedom from fear—anywhere in the world." The speech inspired Rockwell. At first the government rejected his offer to create paintings on the "Four Freedoms" theme, using four scenes of everyday American life. But *The Saturday Evening Post*, one of the nation's most popular magazines, commissioned and reproduced the paintings. Thereafter they served as the centerpiece of a massive U.S. war bond drive.

BELOW: The U.S Treasury believed that posters conveying a "personal appeal" were the most effective. The image of the soldier throwing a grenade in this poster was thought to have this "personal appeal." The artist was Bernard Perlin, who during the war worked for *Life* and *Fortune* magazines.

OPPOSITE PAGE: A Ferdinand Warren poster selling war bonds. Like Soviet posters, U.S. propaganda art liked to portray massed armaments on the ground and in the air. Far from being fantasy, this was an accurate representation of American military might in the last two years of the war.

Books cannot be killed by fire.

People die, but books never die. No man and no force can put thought in a concentration camp forever. No man and no force can take from the world the books that embody man's eternal fight against tyranny. In this war, we know, books are weapons. *Franklin D Roosevelt*

BOOKS ARE WEAPONS IN THE WAR OF IDEAS

FOR ADDITIONAL COPIES WRITE, DIVISION OF PUBLIC INQUIRY, OFFICE OF WAR INFORMATION, WASHINGTON, D. C. SPECIFY O. W. I. NO. 1.

Americans!
SHARE THE MEAT
as a wartime necessity

To meet the needs of our armed forces and fighting allies, a Government order limits the amount of meat delivered to stores and restaurants.

To share the supply fairly, all civilians are asked to limit their consumption of beef, veal, lamb, mutton and pork to 2½ lbs. per person per week.

YOUR FAIR WEEKLY SHARE

Men, women and children over 12 yrs. old . . . . **2½** Pounds per week

Children 6 to 12 yrs. old . . . . **1½** Pounds per week

Children under 6 yrs. old . . . . **¾** Pound per week

You can add these foods to your share: liver, sweetbreads, kidneys, brains and other variety meats; also poultry and fish.

HELP WIN THE WAR!
Keep within your share

FOODS REQUIREMENT COMMITTEE
War Production Board

Claude R. Wickard
Chairman

OWI Poster No. 10. Additional copies may be obtained upon request from the Division of Public Inquiries, Office of War Information, Washington, D.C.

OPPOSITE PAGE: In May 1933, German students in 34 university towns burned 25,000 books by 200 authors in an "Action Against the Un-German Spirit." Under Nazi influence the students claimed they were cleansing the national character of Jewish and other foreign influences. Ten years later this poster was produced carrying President Roosevelt's views on book burning. The message was clear: the United States was fighting a just war in defense of freedom of

ABOVE: In the spring of 1942, the Food Rationing Program was established. Thereafter foodstuffs were rationed, with meats, butter, fat, and oils being the most restricted. Rationing resulted in one serious side effect—the black market, where people could buy rationed items at high prices. For the most part, black marketeers dealt in meat, sugar, and gasoline in the United States.

BELOW: This poster announces free activities, such as movies, concerts. exhibits, and tours, at the American Museum of Natural History, New York. During the war every state provided free leisure activities to maintain public morale. Hollywood stars, especially leading ladies, also did their bit to aid the war effort, donating their time and money in events across the country.

OPPOSITE PAGE: In this poster Adolf Hitler is caricatured in a riposte to German propaganda that tried to convince the Americans that democracy and their armed forces were weak. Hitler is illustrated as a comical buffoon, not to be taken seriously. In general, American posters did not dehumanize their German foes, one of the reasons being that many Americans were of European descent. To dehumanize Europeans would be to dehumanize themselves.

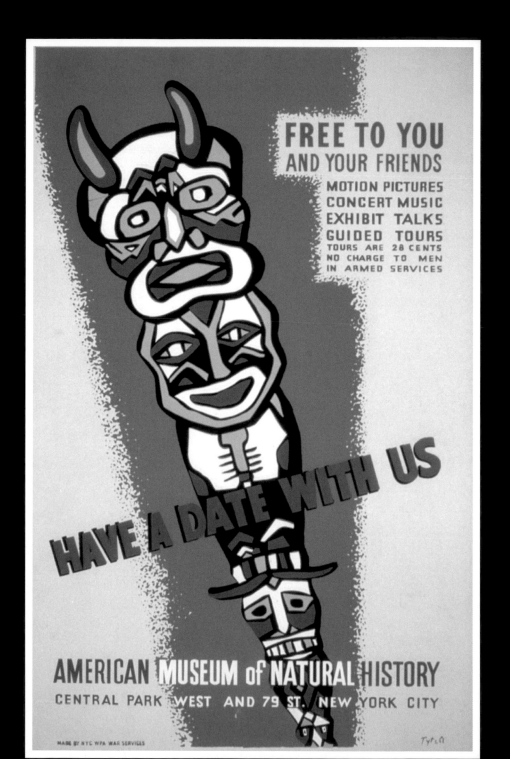

HITLER WANTS US TO BELIEVE THAT:

- Democracy is dying.
- Our armed forces are weak.
- The "New Order" is inevitable.
- Jews cause everybody's troubles, everywhere.
- We are lost in the Pacific.
- Our West Coast is in such grave danger there is no point in fighting on.
- The British are decadent, and "sold us a bill of goods."
- Some sort of "peace" can be made with Nazi Germany.
- The cost of the war will bankrupt the nation.
- Civilian sacrifices will be more than we can bear.
- Our leaders are incompetent; our Government incapable of waging war.

- Stalin is getting too strong, and Bolshevism will sweep over Europe.
- Aid to our allies must stop.
- This is a "white man's war"; our real peril is the Japanese, and we must join Germany to stamp out the "Yellow Peril."
- We must bring all our troops and weapons back to the United States, and defend only our own shores.
- The Chinese, the British, and the Russians will make separate peace with Japan and Germany.
- American democracy will be lost during the war: the two-party system is dead; Congressional elections will never again be held.

THE BRITISH BZ-Z-Z Z-Z-Z-Z-Z

THE AMERICANS BZ-Z-Z Z-Z-Z-Z-Z

AMERICANS WILL NOT BE FOOLED!

U. S. GOVERNMENT PRINTING OFFICE : 1943—O—476339

BELOW: The government wanted a healthy population, which meant a healthy workforce and healthy recruits for the armed forces. However, a major problem was that rationing meant an enormous change in eating habits. Protein was in short supply, as meat, fish, poultry, eggs, and cheese were rationed. Many Americans found it very difficult to adjust to the enormous change in eating habits brought on by rationing.

OPPOSITE PAGE: Preventative measures were encouraged during the war. This poster highlights the potential health risks from exposure to flies. House flies may spread diseases such as conjunctivitis, poliomyelitis, typhoid fever, tuberculosis, anthrax, leprosy, cholera, diarrhea, and dysentery. Flies can also transmit diseaes to animals such as cattle, swine, and poultry.

DON'T

WASTE

WATER

PHILADELPHIA COUNCIL OF DEFENSE

PENNA ART WPA

OPPOSITE PAGE: This poster promotes sewing as a contribution to the war effort. Every activity, no matter how trivial or seemingly unimportant, was linked to the war effort. As President Roosevelt said in 1942: "One front and one battle where everyone in the United States—every man, woman, and child—is in action. That front is right here at home, in our daily lives."

ABOVE: Raymond Wilcox created this simple poster for the Pennsylvania Works Progress Administration (WPA). In World War II, some 9.9 million citizens lived in Pennsylvania. It was estimated that if each of them drank an average of 4.2 gallons (two liters) of water per day, then they would consume almost five million gallons (20 million liters) daily. People were therefore encouraged to save water by fixing leaky faucets, turning off the water while lathering up when shaving, and recycling bath water for use in the garden.

OPPOSITE PAGE: The consumption of healthy foods was seen as a vital part of the effort on the home front. A government pamphlet printed in 1944 stated: "The slogan in this war has been 'Food Is a Weapon of War—As Important as Guns and Ammunition!' In response American farmers have planted more acreage, especially to high-nutrient crops like soybeans and peanuts, raised more livestock, particularly hogs, and produced more dairy products—cheese, butter, and eggs needed by our allies. Despite a shortage of labor and machinery, but with the help of very favorable climate, 1942 agricultural production, including crops, livestock, and livestock products, rose 24 per cent and 1943 production 29 per cent above that of the average years 1935–39."

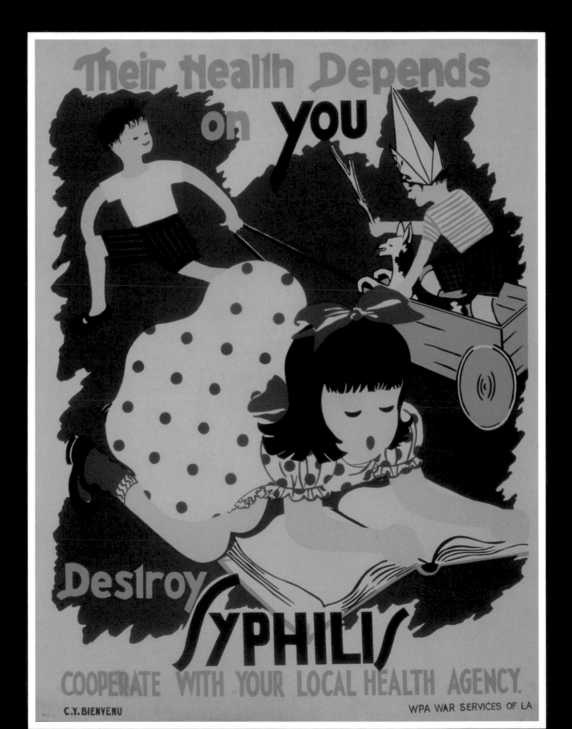

EAT
THESE EVERY DAY

MILK – a pint for adults – more for children cheese or evaporated milk or dried milk **ORANGES** tomatoes grapefruit – raw cabbage or salad greens at least one of these **VEGETABLES** green or yellow – some raw some cooked **FRUITS** in season also dried and canned fruit **BREAD** and cereal – whole grain products or enriched white bread and white flour **MEAT** poultry fish – dried beans peas or nuts **EGGS** – 3 or 4 a week cooked any way you choose or used in prepared dishes – **BUTTER** vitamin rich fats and peanut butter Then eat any other foods you may choose

MADE BY NYC WPA WAR SERVICES

This is your **AIR RAID**
PROTECTION

Get it **NOW**

SAND

FIRST AID

PENNSYLVANIA STATE COUNCIL OF DEFENSE
CAPITOL BUILDING, HARRISBURG, PA. ★

OPPOSITE PAGE: As well as posters calling for Victory Gardens, state authorities printed pamphlets that contained "Fifteen Steps for the Individual Victory Gardener to Follow." They contained advice such as: "Choose a site which is reasonably level and well exposed to sun and air movement. One might not recommend the latter in Western Kansas or Oklahoma, but in the humid Northeastern States good air circulation is desirable."

ABOVE: During the early part of the war most Americans believed that the United States would be bombed. Indeed, when asked by a reporter if the U.S. was open to enemy attack, President Roosevelt replied, "Enemy ships could swoop in and shell New York; enemy planes could drop bombs on war plants in Detroit; enemy troops could attack Alaska." When the reporter enquired as to whether the army, navy, and the air force were strong enough to repulse such attacks, Roosevelt replied, "Certainly not."

BELOW: A poster produced for the Office of Special Services in March 1943. At this time the Philippines was under Japanese occupation, and this intensely patriotic poster was designed to boost Filipino morale. During the occupation the Filipino resistance was extremely active, with around 260,000 people in guerrilla organizations fighting the Japanese. Their effectiveness was such that by the end of the war, Japan controlled only 12 of the 48 provinces in the Philippines.

OPPOSITE PAGE: One of the most sophisticated examples of atrocity propaganda that came out of the war. This poster by Karl Koehler and Victor Ancona won the first prize in the "Nature of the Enemy" section of the U.S. Artists for Victory competition in 1942. Interestingly, it uses a stereotype of the monocled Prussian officer that dated back to the propaganda images of World War I.

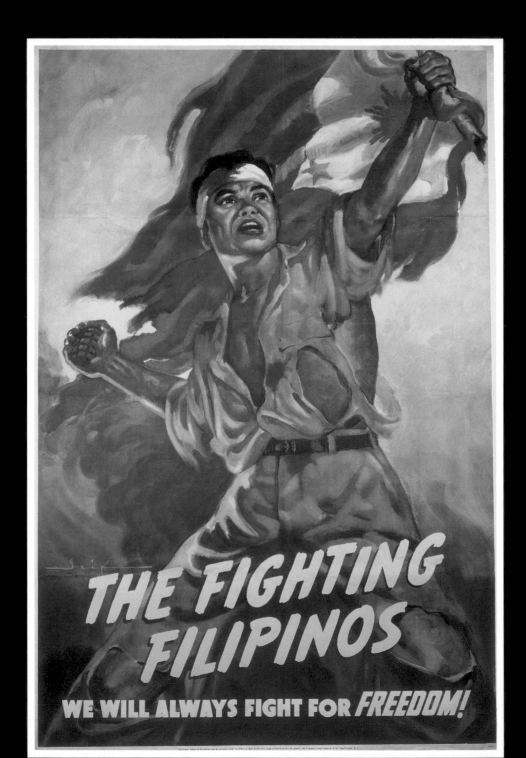

This is the Enemy

OPPOSITE PAGE: United China Relief was founded in 1941 when five different American relief organizations merged to aid the people of China. The aim of the organization was to ease the suffering of the sick and refugees, provide aid for wounded Chinese servicemen, and also to guerrilla units fighting the Japanese in China. Note how the artist, Martha Sawyers, has softened the Oriental features of the Chinese family in the picture. The young child could almost pass for an all-

ABOVE: In contrast, this poster depicts the Japanese as rats, who will be exterminated just as one kills pests in the home. The notion that the enemy was less than human made it easier to kill him. Films were regularly shown to service personnel that promoted this image of the enemy. *Our enemy: the Japanese*, produced in 1943 by the U.S. Office of War Information, Bureau of Motion Pictures, was used to increase hatred against the Japanese within the armed forces. The narration

Index